Landscapes of the
SOUTHERN
PELOPONNESE

a countryside guide
Second edition

Michael Cullen

SUNFLOWER BOOKS

Copyright © 2014
Sunflower Books™
PO Box 36160
London SW7 3WS, UK
www.sunflowerbooks.co.uk

Sunflower Books and
'Landscapes' are
Registered Trademarks.

ISBN 978-1-85691-451-2

Lizard and anemones

Important note to the reader

We have tried to ensure that the descriptions and maps in this book are error-free at press date. The book will be updated, where necessary, whenever future printings permit. It will be very helpful for us to receive your comments (sent in care of the publishers, please) for the updating of future printings.

We also rely on those who use this book — especially walkers — to take along a good supply of common sense when they explore. Conditions can change fairly rapidly in the Peloponnese, and *storm damage or bulldozing may make a route unsafe at any time*. If the route is not as we outline it here, and your way ahead is not secure, return to the point of departure. *Never attempt to complete a tour or walk under hazardous conditions!* Please read carefully the notes on pages 30 to 36, as well as the introductory comments at the beginning of each tour and walk (regarding road conditions, equipment, grade, distances and time, etc). Explore *safely*, while at the same time respecting the beauty of the countryside.

Cover photograph: Mystras, the Byzantine site (Short walk 19, Car tour 2)
Title page: chapel next to the Koumoundourakis Tower (Walk 7, Car tour 2)

Photographs: pages 75 and 76: Matthew Dean; pages 80, 84 and cover: Shutterstock; all other photographs by Michael Cullen
Maps: Sunflower Books, based on maps of Road Editions and Atrapos, with permission (see page 34)
A CIP catalogue record for this book is available from the British Library.
Printed and bound in England by Short Run Press

❀ Contents

Preface   5
  Acknowledgements; Further reading   6

Getting about   7

Touring   8
  Car tour 1: Pylos and the Koroni/Methoni peninsula   10
  Car tour 2: Mt Taygetus and the outer Mani   13
  Car tour 3: Areopolis and the deep Mani   20
  Car tour 4: Leonidion, Mt Parnon and the Arcadian coast   24
  Car tour 5: Monemvasia and the Vatika Peninsula   27

Walking   30
  The walks   30
  The land and people   30
  Walk wisely   31
  Equipment   32
  Nuisances   33
  Weather   33
  Maps   34
  Suggested bases for walking   35
  Explanatory notes   35
  A note about churches   35
  Glossary   36

  THE WALKS
   1 Around ancient Messene   37
   2 Nestor's Palace • Romanos Beach • Petrohori (or Voidokilia) 40
   3 Golden Beach • Paliokastro • Voidokilia Beach •
     Profitis Ilias • Golden Beach   42
   4 Two short walks near Pylos   45
   5 Kato Karveli • Karveli • Lada • Artemisia   47
   6 Profitis Ilias • Pigadiotiko Bridge • Pigadia •
     (Koskarakas Gorge) • Profitis Ilias   50
   7 Sotirianika • Kambos • (Zarnatas Castle) • Kardamyli   53
   8 Kardamyli • Viros Gorge • Lykaki Monastery • Tseria •
     Exohori • Ayia Sofia • Kardamyli   59
   9 Kardamyli • Petrovouni • Proastio • Kalamitsi Beach •
     Kardamyli   64
  10 Panayia Yiatrissa Monastery • Milia • (Eleohori) •
     Ayios Nikolaos   67
  11 Itilo • Dekoulou Monastery • Neo Itilo Beach • Areopolis •
     Pirgos Dirou Sea-caves   71
  12 Three grassy meadows: Thalames • Somatiana •
     Langada • Thalames   75
  13 Two short walks near Stavri   78
  14 Gerolimenas • Pepon • Leontakis • (Mountanistika) •
     Gerolimenas   80
  15 Paliros • Vathy Bay • Kokkinoyia • Temple of Poseidon •
     Cape Tainaron • Kokkinoyia   83

4 Landscapes of the southern Peloponnese

16 Koumousta • Gholas Monastery • Rasina Valley • Koumousta   86
17 Ascent of Mt Taygetus: Profitis Ilias (Aï Lias) Peak   88
18 Ayios Georgios Chapel • Anavriti • Soha • Kalivia Sohas   91
19 Mystras • Taygeti • Zoodochou Pigis Monastery •
   Pergandeïka • Faneromeni Monastery • Langadiotissa
   Gorge • Mystras   95
20 Mount Parnon — from the EOS mountain refuge to
   Malevis Nunnery   100
21 Polydroso (Tzitzina) • Stamatira summit • Ayii Anargyri
   Monastery • Polydroso   103
22 Leonidion • Melana • Livadi   106
23 Trailhead above Leonidion • Tsitalia • Sintzas Monastery
   • Leonidion   109
24 From Pigadi to Poulithra   113
25 From Kremasti to Kiparissi   116
26 Around Monemvasia   120
27 Ayios Nikolaos • Vavila • Ayia Katerini • Faraklo •
   Mesohori • (Ayia Paraskevi Castle) • Neapoli   122
28 Velanidia • Ayios Pavlos Beach • Kato Kastania   126
29 Velanidia • Ayios Thomas • Cape Maleas lighthouse •
   Velanidia   128
30 Ayia Marina • Ayia Irini • Ayia Marina   130

Transport timetables   133
Index   135
Fold-out touring maps   *inside back cover*

Black pine on Mt Taygetus (Car tour 2)

Preface

For most people, Greece is synonymous with sun-drenched islands and seaside resorts — the kind of lazy holiday where you never stray more than 500 yards from the coast, or 100 yards from your hire car.

But venture inland, away from the crowds, and there are some surprises in store: snow-capped mountains, limestone gorges, shady rivers, crumbling castles, tower-villages, fir forests, frescoed chapels, isolated monasteries. It's a different world, seemingly a thousand miles from the resorts, but in fact just a short bus ride or drive. It is no surprise to learn that some mountain villagers still speak Slav-based dialects which are all Greek to the rest of the nation.

So where is this hidden country? You can find it throughout mainland Greece but, for me, the region which packs the most variety into the smallest space is the Peloponnese. From the beaches of Arcadia to the fir forests of Mt Parnon, from the olive groves of Kalamata to the pyramidal peak of Prophet Elijah, from classical Sparta to medieval Mani, this compact semi-island has it all. Though the ancients called it 'the island of Pelops', after their mythical king, this three-fingered landmass is joined to the mainland by a narrow isthmus at Corinth. Only in the 19th century was a canal finally cut through the isthmus, but it retains the cultural diversity and spectacular scenery of the mainland. It's a rich, colourful, age-old landscape which, in this book, I hope to share with discerning travellers.

Because there's so much to discover, I've drawn an east-west line roughly through the middle of the Peloponnese, and limited myself to the southern half. By good fortune, this contains its highest mountain range (Mt Taygetus), its finest Byzantine chapels and medieval forts (in the Mani), its wildest seascapes (Capes Tainaron and Maleas), its largest forest (Mt Parnon) and, arguably, some of its loveliest beaches (Pylos, Kiparissi and Elafonisos, to name a few).

The book is divided into two sections: car tours and walks. The picnic spots highlighted in the car tours will give you a glimpse of magical places within a short walk of the road, yet far from the noise of the 21st century. Pack some warm bread, juicy tomatoes, crunchy cucumber, feta and olives, not forgetting a bottle of cold water or retsina, and you can have an authentic Greek salad in an authentic Greek setting. We also

Velanidia, the most beautiful village on the Vatika Peninsula (Walks 28 and 29, detour on Car tour 5)

suggest some cafés for a reviving coffee and pastry afterwards. But the greatest emphasis in the book is on walking, which, as well as being a lovely way of unwinding, staying healthy and meeting complete strangers, is often the only way of reaching the most beautiful or historic spots.

Enjoy the Peloponnese!   —MICHAEL CULLEN

Acknowledgements
I would like to thank my father and mother for moving to Greece when I was young, and for giving me such a magical childhood and deep roots in the country; Maike, for her tireless (and sometimes tired) good humour, company and laughter; and all the Greek villagers, shepherds, drivers and sailors who have guided, housed, fed and transported me, wanting nothing more than the warmth of shared humanity, throughout 10 years of exploring rural Greece.
— *Michael Cullen, from the First edition of the book*
Sunflower would like to thank Matthew Dean, who lives in the Mani, for updating this Second edition, checking all routes in the west and contributing a new Walk 12 (the original trail had become impassable). But note that it was not practical for Mat to check all the drives and walks in the east (Car tours 4 and 5, Walks 20-30).

Further reading
For more detailed information on the Peloponnese, the best books are Cadogan's *Greece: the Peloponnese* (Dana Facaros and Linda Theodorou, 2008) and Bradt's *Greece: The Peloponnese* (Andrew Bostock, 2013). Other good guides are *Inside Messinia* by Andrew Bostock (2009) and *Inside the Mani* by Matthew Dean (2006).
An excellent online resource for itineraries and accommodation is www.i-escape.com/greece.
For details on churches and castles in the Mani, John Chapman's http://www.maniguide.info is unbeatable.
For an insight into the Taygetus range, Anavasi's *Taygetos* (T Adamakopoulos and P Matsouka), available locally, is interesting and well illustrated, but not totally reliable.

🌻 Getting about

By far the best way to get about is to hire a **car**; otherwise, the best option is to stay at one or more of the suggested bases (see page 35) and use local transport where necessary.

Buses are reliable and, in most cases, the only way of getting about. Printed timetables are rare, web information not always up-to-date. Your best bet is to refer to pages 133-134 and confirm times in the village bus station or stop (sometimes housed in a café). Most buses leave from the end-of-the-line village around dawn, head to the city and return around lunchtime; some do this twice or more in a day. There are also identical-looking school buses (μαθητικο, mathitikó) which operate similar routes and have been known to pick up stranded tourists. The two main hubs (with secondary hubs in brackets) are Kalamata (Pylos, Itilo) and Sparta (Gythion, Areopolis, Gerolimenas, Neapoli, Monemvasia). The Arcadian coast is served by buses between Argos, Tripolis and Leonidion. Bus stops and shelters are identified by a sign, KTEL (the national bus company: www.ktelbus.gr).

Split four ways, the cost of a **taxi** is about the same as the bus fare. Most villages of a reasonable size have a local taxi (see page 134). Otherwise you can call one out from the nearest town, but you'll have to pay more for the extra mileage. It is worth booking taxis ahead of time, as they often have long-distance trips scheduled into their day. The meter should be switched on to tariff 2 (tariff 1 only applies within city limits), and when you get in will normally show the amount due for the journey made so far. However, for standard journeys in the countryside it is quite common to charge the going rate without switching the meter on.

Trains run from Athens to the Peloponnese (the stretch between Argos and Tripolis being particularly scenic), but these will not get you to any of the tours or walks.

At press date there is a **ferry** service (www.ferries.gr) from Athens/Piraeus down the east coast to Monemvasia (Walk 26) or Neapoli. It sails to Monemvasia on Friday evening and returns on Sunday night. This is one of the most delightful ways of reaching Plaka/Leonidion (Walks 22-24) and Kiparissi (Walk 25), as well as smaller fishing villages like Geraka and Tiros. Some vessels continue to Kythira Island or Kastelli on Crete. For the small island of Elafonisos near Neapoli, you will need to get a ferry or passenger boat (see Car tour 5).

✻ Touring

The Peloponnese has some truly spectacular drives, and a car tour through the area can be a breathtaking experience as well as a useful overview of places you might want to return to for a fuller exploration. Two of Greece's most scenic mountain roads are those across the Taygetus and Parnon ranges, which are covered by Car tours 2 and 4 respectively. Coastal drives form part of every tour, with suggested detours to beautiful and little-visited beaches.

Each of the five car tours is feasible in a day or (better) two; to explore all five thoroughly would take weeks. The tours follow asphalt roads throughout, apart from a few short optional stretches of good dirt road (some of which are due to be asphalted in 2003). There is also a rough dirt road over the southern ranges of Mt Taygetus, which is included as an option on Car tour 2 because of its unrivalled panoramas.

Do remember that hire cars are not normally allowed on **unsurfaced roads**, and that damage to the underside of the car is not covered by the standard insurance policy. The chances of a puncture are also much higher on dirt roads, especially when travelling at speed. Having said that, many of the loveliest spots can only be reached by unsurfaced road, so you will need to use your judgement!

Car hire on mainland Greece is often cheaper when purchased abroad, before travelling. If you hire locally, shop

Old town of Monemvasia (Car tour 5, Walk 26)

around, compare like for like, and don't be afraid to ask for their 'best price'. As always, you should check the petrol level, lights, spare tyre, jack and general condition of the vehicle before driving away in it.

Fuel is reasonably priced and widely available in the Peloponnese, except in mountainous areas. Unleaded (which has replaced leaded almost entirely) is αμολυβδη (amólivthi). Diesel is πετρελαιο (petrélleo), although 'deézell' is also understood. Most petrol stations are staff-served, so don't blithely go helping yourself without checking! Full is γεματο (yemáto). If you have a **puncture**, you'll find tyre repair garages alongside most petrol stations.

Motoring law is similar to other continental European countries, but is flouted more often and more flagrantly. Drive on the right, overtake on the left, and don't count on others being aware of you. Flashing your headlights means 'Watch out for me' (as per the highway code) rather than the British 'After you, old chap'. Drink-driving is, at last, being clamped down on, with fines around 150 Euro. Front seat belts must be worn, and children under 10 must ride in the back. Parking is fairly chaotic, with lots of double parking and few cities outside Athens enforcing restrictions.

Speed limits are generally 50km/h in built-up areas, 80km/h on good country roads, and 120km/h or 130km/h on the motorways. But lower limits may be placed at any point. Police speed traps are quite common on the larger country roads, especially between Sparta and Gythion.

Most importantly, be aware that **road surfaces are poor and unpredictable**, with unsigned potholes and bumps a serious danger at night-time. Unlit tractors and bicycles are also common. If you have an accident, you must stop and exchange details (usually accompanied by a great deal of emotive shouting).

The fold-out touring maps show all the roads followed in the tours, as well as the location of all the walks, suggested picnic spots and other information useful to the curious motorist. **Symbols** used in the text are explained in the map key. Distances in km are given cumulatively, starting from my chosen base (if possible, reset your distance counter when leaving or passing this point). **Detours** (shown in *italic type* in the text) are *not included* in the cumulative distances.

The notes themselves are restricted to route directions, occasional descriptions of the scenery, and very brief asides on the places you pass. For further information on the area and specific sites, see 'Further reading' on page 6; there is also more historical information in the walking notes.

Car tour 1: PYLOS AND THE KORONI/METHONI PENINSULA

Pylos • (Divari • Voidokilia) • (Romanos) • Hora • Petalidi • (Koroni) • (Marathi) • Methoni • Pylos

110km/68mi; 3h driving time, plus up to 56km/35mi (2h) of detours
Opening times:
Nestor's Palace and Hora
Archaeological Museum: Tue-

Sun 08.30-14.30, closed Mon
Koroni Castle: unrestricted entry
Methoni Castle: daily 09.00-19.00
Picnic suggestions: Waterfall near Yialova (detour at 7km); **Koroni Castle** (detour at 75km)

The southwestern finger of the Peloponnese is blessed with some of Greece's most idyllic sandy beaches, not to mention lovely seaside towns, pre-Classical sites and more than its fair share of medieval castles. This day tour combines the best of these and gives you a glimpse of some of the little-visited countryside in between: olive groves, flower-filled meadows, wayside chapels. You'll find some suggestions for short walks, as well as a couple of eye-openers for the adventurous: an unexpected waterfall and a river-gorge spanned by an Ottoman aqueduct. The delightful town of Pylos is an ideal base, allowing you to complete the more 'active' exploration in the relative cool of the morning, leaving the beaches until the afternoon.

From **Pylos★** (🏢🏖✕🍷M🏪) take the KALAMATA road, climbing through the northwestern part of town with good views back over

the port. After 2.5km, at a fork, go left towards GARGALIANI.
*But first, if you are feeling intrepid, you can make a 7km return **detour***

to the Dafnorema river-gorge and aqueduct by forking right towards Kalamata (see Walk 4b on page 45 for directions).

Shortly after **Yialova** (7km 🏨✕ 🚐🅿) you reach a left turn signed 'GOLDEN BEACH 3, VOIDOKILIA'.

For the worthwhile 6km return detour to the Divari Lagoon and Voidokilia Bay★ (🏛), turn left. After 3km, where the asphalt road bears right, continue straight on (slowly — do not run over any chameleons!) and park at the open car park. On your left is the long strand of Golden Beach, facing south into Navarino Bay. A little further ahead is a signed nature trail following a wooden walkway, which introduces you to some of the 255 bird species observed around the Divari Lagoon: egrets, herons, cormorants, terns, black-winged stilts, glossy ibis and flamingoes, to name but a few. The area is also a breeding ground for the endangered African chameleon and loggerhead turtle (Caretta caretta), which is why you are asked not to camp, light fires,

stick parasols into the sand, or disturb nests. If you fancy stretching your legs, Walk 3 starts and ends here, taking in the perfect horseshoe bay of Voidokilia and the ruined medieval castle of Paliokastro, shown on page 43. The bay, which is also accessible from Petrohori to the north, gets very crowded in summer, but is a delight in spring or autumn, or in the early morning at any time of year.

Just 100m north of the turning to Golden Beach and just south of the Shell garage, you reach a right turn signed 'SHINOLAKA 3'.

Here you can make a 5km return detour to the waterfall of Yialova (see Walk 4a on page 45 for directions). The waterfall, which normally flows from March to June, makes a refreshing spot for a picnic (P; photograph page 46).

The main tour continues north towards Hora for 5km, to a right-hand bend (12km) signed 'KYPARISSIA 49' (right) and 'ROUMANOU 2' (left).

For a 5km return detour to Romanos Beach (Paralia Romanou), turn left and then keep right, signed ROMANOS. After 0.8km, turn left (ROMANOS, PETROHORI), and after 0.5km, just before Romanos village, fork right (white on blue arrow). A road soon joins from the left (from Romanos centre); keep right (sign: TO BEACH) and head southwest for 1.2km. At the coast, turn left for a small, tamarisk-shaded beach (✕ 🅿); or turn right on a dirt road, past a protected cove, to the beginning of a long, sandy beach stretching north as far as the eye can see.

After the turning to Romanos, the next left turn leads to the very grand Costa Navarino hotel and golf course. But the main tour continues northeast towards Hora, winding up through olive groves,

The horseshoe bay of Voidokilia, backed by the Divari Lagoon

past the turning to Korifasio, the site of ancient Pylos. After 5km you pass **Nestor's Palace** on the left (17km 🏛), the best-preserved example — thanks to a cataclysmic fire which buried the place in ash — of a Mycenean royal residence. Using tablets found here, Ventris and Chadwick were able to decipher the ancient language 'Linear B'. Walk 2 leads from here, past olive groves and Mycenean tombs, to Romanos Beach.

The road straightens out and enters the authentic provincial town of **Hora** (20km 🎬🅿M🚻), with its lively central square. Pass the Archaeological Museum and leave the main Kyparissia road, following signs to 'KALAMATA 50'. You climb a hill to the village of **Metamorfosi** (27km), carry on straight over the crossroads known as TOULOUPA HANI (29km), and down the other side. Continue up to a left turn, which you ignore, followed by a right turn (32km), which you take. Pass the village of **Vlasi** (35km) and keep left through **Kourtaki** (nothing to do with the famous retsina, sadly). At **Drosia** (40km), keep right, past the villages of **Daras** and **Dafni**, to the main KALAMATA–PYLOS ROAD at **Rizomilos** (50km 🚻). Here, turn right and immediately left, towards KORONI.

For the next 20km to Nea Koroni you skirt the rapidly developing coastline (🏖🚻) of cafés, hotels and uninspiring beaches, passing through **Petalidi** (where you go round the square towards 'Κορωνι'), **Kalamaki**, **Hrani**, **Episkopi** and **Ayios Andreas** en route. After **Nea Koroni** (70km) you head inland, bypassing Vounaria and Kombi, to a T-junction in **Harokopio** (75km).

Here you can take a 9km return **detour to Koroni** *(🏖🚻): turn left and, at the fork after 2.3km, a right turn leads to the lovely, sandy beach of Memi (also called Zagha), while left will take you into Koroni town. It is worth strolling through its narrow alleys up to the castle★ (🚻P), within whose solid walls are a delightful chapel, some houses and fine views over the coast to the south.*

To continue the main tour, turn right towards FINIKOUNDA. A new road whisks you up over a 300m pass (📷) near **Yamia** and down past **Akritohori** (84km).

At the T-junction after Akritohori you can leave the new road and seek out one of the loveliest coves on this part of the peninsula by making a 28km return **detour to Marathi Beach***. Follow the old road up towards Chrysokellaria, then, after 4km, turn right down a small road signed to TSAPI. After 8km the asphalt runs out (but may be extended), and just after this there is an unsigned right turn and layby. If you don't have a jeep, I advise parking here and walking. The right fork bumps down for 2km to a pair of sandy beaches separated by a rocky headland. In summer Marathi is popular with free campers, some of whom leave rubbish behind.*

To continue back to Pylos, follow the road down to **Finikounda** (88km 🏖🚻), a once-sleepy fishing village now packed with sun-loving tourists in summer. If it's not too busy, you can drive through the laid-back resort for a drink or a swim, and rejoin the road further up. It whisks you rapidly to **Methoni** (100km 🏖🚻), keeping right of the town centre. If you haven't already seen it, the wonderfully preserved Venetian castle★ (🏛) and seatower are definitely worth driving through town for — endless amusement for children, with a sandy beach and tavernas nearby to complete the fun. Otherwise continue north, past **Kainouryio Horio**, to **Pylos** (110km).

Car tour 2: MT TAYGETUS AND THE OUTER MANI

Kardamyli • Kambos • (Gaïtses) • Kalamata • Artemisia • Mystras • (Anavriti) • Sparta • Xirokambi • (Koumousta) • Egies (Alternative return route) • Gythion • Areopolis • Milia • Kardamyli

235km/146mi; 6h driving time (or 204km/126mi; 6h via the Alternative return route) — plus detours

Walks en route: 5, (6), 7, 8, 9, 10, 11, (16, 17), 18, 19

Opening times:

Mystras Site: daily 08.30-15.00 (17.30 in summer)

Sparta Archaeological Museum: Tue-Sat 08.30-15.00, Sun 10.00-14.00; closed Mon. Site: free entry

All monasteries: mornings and late afternoons only (for Dekoulou Monastery afternoons are best).

Picnic suggestions: Nedon River (55km), **Mystras Castle** (89km), cave-chapel of **Langadiotissa** (detour from Parori at 95km), **Kalivia Sohas** — the church or watchtower (108km), **Koumousta** (a detour after 115km), **Sotiros Chapel** (after 180km), **Vaidenitsa Monastery** (on the Alternative return route after 188km)

This must be one of the most spectacular and varied circuits in Greece. Wonderful coastal scenery is followed by a forested mountain pass; the cities of Sparta and Kalamata contrast with the remote stone villages of the Outer Mani; a dramatic limestone gorge opens out onto a lush plain full of olive and citrus groves. If you have a jeep, or are happy to chance it in a hire car, I highly recommend the alternative return route across the southern Taygetus ridge — it is absolutely breathtaking. Other suggested detours and 'long-cuts' can add up to 58km to the total. Although you *could* complete it in a day, this tour really needs two-three days to take in all the natural splendour. If you start from Stoupa or Kardamyli, you could overnight in Sparta, a lively city, or Mystras, a tranquil village, both one-third of the way around, and then in Gythion, a laid-back seaside town two-thirds of the way round.

Picnic by the upper gate of Mystras Castle

From **Kardamyli** (✝🏔✕🚌🚐);
Walks 7-9) follow the main road
north out of the village towards
KALAMATA, referring to the map on
page 55 for more detail. You wind
up past the villages of **Kalives** and
Prosilio, with impressive views
back over the coast, to a 450m
pass. Then, descending into the
dhemos of Avia, you see the ruined
castle of Zarnatas on a hilltop
ahead. Pass the turn-off right to
Androumbevitsis Monastery and,
500m further on (13.4km),
opposite a bus shelter and shrine,
turn right up a small concrete lane
(unsuitable for wide vehicles) with
a blue sign, 'MALTA'. You pass
below the tower of **Koumoundourakis**, through **Malta** village,
and come to a left bend with a
brown sign 'CHURCH OF THE
ZOODOCHOS PIGI'. **Zarnatas
Castle** (📷; photograph page 57)
is a worthwhile 15-minute climb
from here, offering magnificent
views over Kambos to Taygetus.
See Walk 7 for details on this and
other sites mentioned in this
paragraph.
Carry on down the narrow lane
through **Stavropigio** village and,
at the main road (14.9km 🚌),
turn right. The road winds down,
passing a brown sign to a **Mycenean *tholos* Tomb** (16km), five
minutes' walk to your left, behind
the roofless mansion of Koumoundouros. You enter **Kambos** village
(✝✕🚐; photograph page 56)
and pass the church of Ayii Theodorii on your left, followed by a
dangerous 90° left bend. Just
100m after this, the first right
turn, unsignposted (16.8km),
leads up to Gaïtses village.

***Optional detour to Gaïtses and the
Koskarakas Gorge** (20km/40min
return): follow this road past the
huge parish church, out of Kambos,
past the left turn to Orovas, and up
two sections of zigzags, with a
mysterious crater visible to your right*
*(probably a collapsed cave system). At
a blue sign, KENDRO (7.6km), fork
left into Vorio, which means 'north',
because it is the northernmost of the
four constituent villages of Gaïtses.
Referring to the map on page 52, at
the square go around the church.
Behind it there is a café where you
can ask about the key to Profitis Ilias
church, shown on page 51. From
here, continue along a narrow lane,
forking right by a small blue sign,
FARAGI (gorge). The road becomes a
gravel lane (8.2km), which you
might prefer to walk along. At 9km,
by a telephone pole, a trail winds up
to the chapel of Profitis Ilias on your
left (📷); or you can get similarly
wonderful views over the Koskarakas
Gorge 200m further on. Walk 6
explores this section of the gorge.
Return to Kambos the same way, or
via the Anatoliko (east) and Kendro
/Hora (centre/main) parts of Gaïtses
village (some dirt road).*

The main tour continues directly
north from Kambos. Ignore a left
turn to Santava Beach (17.3km)
and wind down through imma-
culate olive groves to cross the dry
Koskarakas River. The road climbs
again, passing the turn-off right to
Sotirianika (22.2km), where Walk
7 begins. Beyond the hilltop castle
of **Kapetanakos**, you descend (the
bends are slippery when wet) to
join the coast road from Kitries
(29.5km 🚐).
At the outskirts of **Kalamata**
(✝🏔✕🚐⊕M🚌), I suggest
ignoring the left turn to the
seafront (32.7km) and going
straight through town, following
signs to 'SPARTI'. Eventually you
should find yourself driving
parallel to the dry, concreted
watercourse of the river Nedon,
past the bus station (37.8km), and
bearing right to leaving the city.
As the road climbs through
scrubby foothills, keep left where
indicated (blue sign 'SPARTI 55').
After a right bend (46.1km) you

Cave-chapel in the Langadiotissa Gorge (Walk 19); Soha, on the eastern flanks of Taygetus (Walk 18; right)

pass the sharp right turn to 'KATO KARVELI 1.5KM' — the somewhat unlikely start of Walk 5. The main road then zigzags down into the deep Nedon Valley, with its dense covering of bushes, past the right turn to Karveli and Lada, the left turn to Nedousa (55km *P*; some nice riverside spots near here) and up again to the village of **Artemisia** (61km), straddling a spur alongside the road. There are several tavernas and cafés selling mountain tea, fresh yoghurt and honey; and stands selling wooden artefacts and royal jelly. It feels like a different world from the coast. Walk 5 ends here.

Leave the village, ignoring the right turn (65.8km) to 'Lada 6, Karveli 10' and the left turns to Neohori etc. The road winds ever upwards — in winter snowdrifts can cut it off for days — to the 1300m **Langada Pass** (☎), with its forlorn-looking 'motel'. The descent which follows is truly breathtaking. It starts by winding down through partly burnt pine and fir forests, past a mountain hotel and into Laconia province. Bearing left, it follows the left bank of the **Langada Gorge**★ through short tunnels and overhangs, before crossing the watercourse and climbing slightly to the village of **Tripi** (86.1km 🏠 ✖). Here you can park by the Hotel Keadas and follow the steps up the opposite (right) bank to the Καιαδας sinkhole (10min return), into which the Spartans allegedly hurled their criminals, and from which the Messinian rebel-leader

Aristomenes made his miraculous escape in the 7th century BC. Continue towards Sparta for 1km; then, after a right bend with a mirror on the left, fork right up an inconspicuous road signed to Μυστρας. Leave Tripi, continue through **Pikoulianika** (✖) and soon the Byzantine hilltown of Mystras appears ahead, with modern Sparta below and left. At the T-junction (88.9km), turn right for the upper (castle) entrance to the **Mystras site**★ (🏛🏺📷*P*), with its superb views up to Taygetus. There is a lovely short walk from Mystras to this entrance, returning through the site (see Short walk 19; map and photograph on pages 96 and 97). Return to the junction and turn right; at the stop sign by the lower entrance, turn left. A one-way system takes you through the modern village of **Mystras** (🏠✖🏪), to the plane tree at its centre (93.8km). Here turn right, ignore the right fork at the start of **Parori** (94.3km) and ignore (for the time being) the left turn to 'Sparti' (94.6km). You reach a delightful plane-shaded square (94.8km ✖) gushing with spring water — near the end point of Walk 19. If you fancy a magical stroll, follow the signed trail up the valley just beyond the square, to the tranquil cave-chapel of **Langadiotissa** (30min return; ***P***). I could not imagine a more enchanting picnic spot than the chapel surrounds. See page 99 to learn more about its history.

For a spectacular, belly-churning drive, take a ***detour up the tightly-hairpinned road to the mountain village of Anavriti*** *(19km return; ⛰✕). From Parori follow the road south to Ayios Ioannis (see map page 91), and by its clay-coloured church turn right to 'Αναβρυτη 8'. Keep right and start winding up the steep flank of Mt Taygetus. After the second left hairpin you pass the trail-head for Walk 18 (signpost), above the chapel of Ayios Georgios. Soon you lose count of the hairpins, and after 8km arrive at the village square, with a simple hotel on your left and a café ahead. See also pages 92-93.*

The main tour continues to Sparta: from Parori head back (north) for 200m and turn right (95km). You join the MYSTRAS ROAD, drive along a tree-lined avenue, bear left across a bridge and then right into the centre of **Sparta** (⛰✕⛽⊕M ☕). You pass a photo shop on the left run by Vassilis Georgiadis, a helpful English-speaking member of the EOS (Alpine Club), which has its offices on a nearby side road. Just after the huge town square, you reach a busy roundabout (100km), with the ancient site (Π) 1km to your left. Turn right along the main road towards GYTHION and leave town. At the start of Amykles, just before a petrol station (105km ⛽), there is a left turn to the Sanctuary of Apollo (Π), an interesting Mycenean site and mythical tomb of Hyakinthos, which lies 1km off the road (keep left after the houses of Peristeri along a paved lane).

The main tour continues into the centre of **Amykles** (105.5km), where you turn right to KALIVIA SOHAS, keeping left after 400m. In **Kalivia Sohas** (107.2km M☕), turn left and drive through the centre, to a track and playground on the right (107.7km). For another short walk, park here and follow the blue square waymarks to the right (west) up a track, then a paved path, to the church of Zoodochou Pigis (5min; ***P***). Behind the church the trail continues, forking left onto a stepped path, up to the crumbling medieval watchtower (12min; 📷***P***) which once guarded the route up the mountain (Walk 18). Either of these buildings would make a lovely picnic spot, the former shady and protected, the latter sunny and panoramic.

Driving south from Kalivia, you reach the larger village of **Anoyia** (111km ☕), where the road jinks right and then left.

Possible short detour: *At the cross-roads, you could turn right, initially towards 'Socha 13', then keep left after 1.7km, to the monastery of* ***Panayia Katafighiotissa*** *—Virgin Mary of the Refuge. Another dramatic and spiritual spot, the church and outbuildings sit, dominated by cliffs, at the entrance of a cave where once the Orthodox faithful took refuge from their Ottoman persecutors.*

From Anoyia, the road continues south, almost seamlessly, into the next village of **Paleopanayia** (112.5km ✕☕), with its fine two-storey houses and small tourist information centre (usually closed). Ignore the right turn to the EOS mountain refuge (start of Walk 17), and the left turn to Τραπεζοντη, and continue straight on to **Xirokambi** (115km ⛽☕), where the shady square is lined with enticing pastry shops.

At the beginning of the square, by a cardphone, you can make an ***exciting***

Gythion harbour, with octopus drying above a waterside café

detour to Koumousta (14km return; P): turn right, followed by a left and a right. This near-deserted village is set among high cliffs, with the obligatory plane tree and gushing spring at the upper square — a charming spot for a picnic, where Walk 16 begins and ends.

The main tour continues straight through Xirokambi, across the bridge and, ignoring turn-offs to Anthohori and Paleohori, reaches **Dafni**. At the start of this village a right turn winds up to the walled nunnery of Zerbitsa in 3km, but you may have seen enough monasteries for the time being, so carry on to the next fork (117.2km). Here, keeping right (straight) would take you up tortuous minor roads, through the Vardounohoria (villages of the Vardounia valleys) and down again to Gythion. Apart from the usual mountain views and one lovely village square (in Arna), there is nothing particular to recommend it, so I advise forking left towards the 'NATIONAL ROAD 6', and getting some miles (or kilometres) under your belt. In **Potamia** keep left to reach the main SPARTA–GYTHION ROAD at around the 123km-mark. Turn right and, keeping an eye out for police speed traps, drive south, past the left turn to Krokees and

Monemvasia, all the way to **Egies** (138km 🚌). At the end of this linear village, there is a right turn signed, among others, to the villages of Ayios Nikolaos and Kastania. This is the start of the **Alternative return route** over the southern ridge of Taygetus, crossing a spectacular 1600m pass with panoramic views, fir forests — and 27km of *unsurfaced* road (see overleaf).

The main tour continues to **Gythion** (145km 🚶🏨🍴🅿️M⛴). As you enter the town, keep right to reach the picturesque seafront, which is invariably jammed with tourists, shoppers, taxis, cruising motorbikes, fishmongers' vans and police cars double-parked outside their station. A quayside drink or bite of grilled octopus guarantees entertainment, especially if the weekly ferry from Crete arrives at the same time. Park at the very beginning of the waterfront if you can.

Continue around the roundabout, follow the quayside to the right (more parking), pass the islet of Marathonisi (**M**; well-presented museum on the legendary spot where Paris and Helen set sail for Troy) and leave town. The road heads inland — though beaches and campsites are never far away to your left — and through the small **Passava Gorge**, whose left flank is topped by a ruined Frankish castle (▮). After the gorge (♟), follow the road left; a small brown sign indicates an overgrown track leading up to said castle. At 158km a road joins from the left, signed 'Skoutari 6' and Kotronas. Here you briefly join Car tour 3; see the last paragraphs on page 23 for additional detail en route to Areopolis and, if you plan to go southwards to the Deep Mani, see page 20.

At the entrance to **Areopolis** (171km ♦▲✕♟⊕▮; Walk 11) turn sharp right towards 'KARDA-MYLI 45' etc. A couple of bends bring views over the gulf of Itilo. At 174.6km I suggest you turn sharp left into the fishing village of Limeni (excellent seafood taverna and the mansion of Petrobey Mavromichalis) before rejoining the main road at **Neo Itilo** (Tsipa; ▲✕▮) 1km further on. The beach here is one of the few sandy strands in the Mani, but often spoiled by incoming debris and murky water. The road then climbs in a huge hairpin (☞), with fine views back over the gulf. An interesting route (see map on page 73) is to turn sharp right just before the righthand hairpin, opposite a bus shelter (180km). At the fork after 0.6km, the concrete lane to the right leads down to the camouflaged monastery of **Dekoulou**, whose marvellously frescoed chapel may be opened for you by the children from the adjacent house (afternoons are best). Walk 11 passes here en route to Areopolis; follow it backwards (east) to Sotiros Chapel for a lovely picnic spot (*P*; photograph page 72). To continue to Itilo, keep left at the fork. At the central square (▮) follow the main road left, past a larger, paved square (✕), to a T-junction with the road from

Karea. Turn left, leave the village and at the main road (183km ▲) turn right towards Καλαματα. The road follows the rocky western flanks of **Ayios Nikon** mountain, speckled with small oak trees. You enter **Messinia** (ignore the left turn to Hotasia), squeeze through **Ayios Nikon** (191km ♦▮) and pass two villages en route in Walk 12: **Langada** (♦▮) and **Thalames** (♦▮ and disappointing private **M** of the Mani). **Nomitsis** (♦) village follows quickly. The beautiful roadside chapels are mostly locked, sadly. Approaching **Platsa**, *leave* the coastal road: at a slight left bend (200.1km) fork right towards 'Μηλεα'. Continue past **Kivelia**, where you keep left to skirt the village. At the first houses of **Milia** (206.4km ▮) keep left to the square, with its pretty church and tower; Walk 10 passes through here on its way down to the coast. Continue straight on (you can see Yiatrissa monastery looking like a giant observatory atop the ridge ahead), past a left bend and out of the valley. You reach the hamlet of **Kariovouni** (also called Arachova; 211km ▮), hidden in a deep valley coming down from Mavrovouni. At the T-junction, turn left (215.5km) and follow the road down through **Pirgos** (▮) and **Neohori** (▮) to the main road (222.5km). Here turn right, past three left turns to Stoupa (▲✕♟ ▮), and follow the scenic coastal road past the tiny cove of **Foneas** (226.5km), back to **Kardamyli** (235km).

Alternative return across the southern Taygetus ridge: from Egies to Kardamyli

(58km; 2h30min driving time)
If you decide to risk this mostly unsurfaced route in a hire car, check at one of the villages (or check before you leave the hotel)

that the road is still passable:
'Περναει ο δρομος μεχρι
Σαιδωνα (με τετοιο αυτοκινητο)?
*Pernáï o dhrómos méhri Saidhóna
(mé tétyo aftokínito)?*
Does the road go through as far as
Saidhona (with a car like this)?'

From the main road in **Egies**
(138km) follow the signed road
west towards AYIOS NIKOLAOS, etc.
The road passes below Archontiko
(ignore right turns), climbs to
Melissa (ignore left turn), wiggles
below the pretty hamlet of
Kokkina Louria and enters the
sizeable village of **Ayios Nikolaos**
(152km ■■▣). Here you can stop
for a drink at the pretty square; 10
minutes' walk up a track from the
northeast corner of the square
stands a ruined Venetian *kastro*, on
a crag overlooking the Vardounia
Valley. From the 15th to the 19th
century, and most famously in
Ibrahim Pasha's defeat at
Polyaravos, the fortress played a
key role in defending the Yiatrissa
pass into the Mani.

Continuing from the square, the
road curls leftwards, passes above
Selegoudi and climbs to **Kastania**
(159km ▣), which means 'chestnut' and is pronounced, unusually,
with the emphasis on the second
'a'. Four kilometres further on you
crest the bleak, windswept ridge
by the huge, unprepossessing
monastery of **Panayia Yiatrissa**
(163km). Walk 10 begins here and
descends to Milia, visible in the
valley below.

The road, now unsurfaced but due
to be asphalted 'soon', continues
just west of the ridge, then winds
up into the fir forest. Look back
for stunning views (📷) over the
pyramidal peaks of Zizali. Ten
kilometres beyond Yiatrissa you
reach a transverse ridge and a
junction (173km).

Detour: *If you branch right for a few
kilometres, you reach the lovely,*

*Mavrovouni peak, from the Vassiliki
Forest*

*forested bowl of **Vassiliki** — ideal
picnicking and hiking country.*
To continue the main tour, branch
left and follow the deteriorating
road across the southern flanks of
Mavrovouni. Wind steeply down
a valley, ignoring the left fork after
9km. When you reach an oblique
junction below the inconspicuous
ruin of **Ayios Samouil** monastery
(188km), you have a choice of
routes.*
For the quickest route back to
Kardamyli, turn right here, following a surprisingly wide and
impressive 'motorway' below the
white-washed monastery of
Vaidenitsa (also called Vodonitsa;
P). The building is now renovated
for hikers and is a lovely picnic
spot if you don't mind the steep
10-minute walk up. You pass a
crag-top tower and continue down
to **Exohori**. This scattered village
has many interesting churches and
enticing mulepaths (see Walk 8).
Turn left along the main road
(194km) and follow it through
Proastio (Walk 9) to the coastal
road by **Kalamitsi Beach**
(202km; Walk 9). Then head
right, back to **Kardamyli**
(204km).

---

*If you want to return to Stoupa,
turn sharp left here into Saïdhona
village (190km). Follow the main
road leftwards, ignoring left turns to
Kastania (this one is pronounced
Kastaniá, as you would expect) and
Milia. Once down on the main
coastal road (202km), turn right to
Stoupa (203km ▲▲✕➤▣).

Car tour 3: AREOPOLIS AND THE DEEP MANI

Areopolis • Pirgos Dirou • Pirgos Dirou Sea-caves • Stavri • Gerolimenas • Vathia • Cape Tainaron • Layia • Kokkala • Kotronas • Skoutari • Areopolis

139km/86mi; 4h driving time, plus 13km/8mi; 20min of detours
Walks en route: 11, (12), 13-15
Opening times/market days:
Pirgos Dirou Sea-caves: 08.00-17.30 (June-Sept); 08.30-14.45 (Oct-May); last entrance 15min before closing. Closed Mondays.
Pirgos Dirou has a Wednesday morning market.
Picnic suggestions: Odigitria Chapel (after 34km), **Vathia** (52km), **Alypa Cove** (after 84km)

This anti-clockwise circuit of the Peloponnese's middle fingertip, designed as a one day tour, shows you the 'Deep Mani' in all its rugged, rocky, sea-washed splendour. Descending the so-called 'shadowy' coast — a fertile, populous plateau west of the mountainous spine of Sangias, and returning via the dramatic corniches of the 'sunward' (eastern) coast, it takes in all the classic sites: tower-villages, sea-caves, medieval castles and Byzantine chapels. I have also included a few of its secret gems, for which you will need to leave your car and walk a short way: a hermit's chapel perched above the sea, a 2000-year-old mosaic circle hidden among the shrubs and a sheltered cove set in a deep inlet.

From **Areopolis** (✝♠✕☐⊕♨; Walk 11) follow the main road south towards PIRGOS DIROU, GEROLIMENAS etc, past the turning to the medical centre and the school, and numerous petrol stations. Ignore the left turn to Kotronas, Nyfi etc (2km) and follow the road past **Kalos** to the junction in the modern village of **Pirgos Dirou** (7km).

Turn right at this junction, past various souvenir stalls, and follow the road right, past the old, stone-built part of the village. The road then bends left and winds down to the **Pirgos Dirou Sea-caves★** (12km ∩M♨ and summer ✕). Park as requested and walk down to the caves, collecting a ticket en route. On summer mornings, especially at weekends, the waiting time may be an hour or two; you can walk north round a rocky headland to a quieter beach (Walk 11 in reverse).

Return to the junction in Pirgos Dirou village (17km) and continue south through **Triantafilia** to a fork (20km). Turn left here ('Δρυαλος 2' etc). You pass through **Drialos** (22km ✝); at the end of the village, on your left, there is a low double-chapel dedicated to Ayios Georgios (open). The left icon shows the eponymous saint on his statutory white horse — there are very strict rules governing the Orthodox depiction of saints — but who is the tiny 'coffee boy' riding pillion? No one knows for sure, but he appears in several local, late-Byzantine churches. A typically Greek explanation is that St George was at a café when he received the divine call to action so, to keep up his strength for the duel with the dragon, he took his undrunk coffee with him, and a boy to carry it. After this there follows a 2km-long stretch of unsurfaced road, due to be asphalted 'soon'. In the village of **Vamvaka** (24km), keep right to reach a crossroads, now referring to the *map inset*.

Ayios Stratigos in Diporo (Walk 14)

A word about visiting the historic chapels en route, most of which you will find locked. In some instances a key is held locally — ask at the café for 'το κλειδί για την εκκλησια …/ *toh klithí ya tin eklisía …*/the key for the church of …', or if you wait outside someone may appear. For the more important churches (Ayios Stratigos, Episkopi etc), you need to find the φυλακας/*filakas* (warden), who at the time of publication is Dimitris Kolokouris, and either travel with him or arrange to meet him en route. Based in Pirgos Dirou, but to be found most mornings in the post office in Areopolis, Dimitris' telephone number is 27330 52953, though he speaks very limited English.

For a (1km return) detour to the chapel of Ayios Theodoros turn left (uphill) here. The house of the key holder is halfway up on your left (grey gate). This decoratively cloisonné chapel uses blocks from an earlier temple, and displays carved marble-work by the local craftsman Nikitas. Unusually, he also carved the date on the western tie-beam inside: 6583 is Byzantine numerals for 1075.

The main tour turns right (downhill) at the crossroads. When you reach the main road (25km), turn left, passing the scattered houses of **Angiadaki** and **Lakkos**.

Shortly after Lakkos there is a small right turn, signed to Erimos. If you are interested in Byzantine chapels, make the (2km return) detour to the chapel of Ayia Varvara or Barbara (recently restored; key locally), to enjoy its harmonious proportions, decorative brickwork and inset ceramic bowls.

Otherwise, continuing south, you flash past the tiny hamlet of **Ayios Georgios** (27km).

Just past Ayios Georgios, a (4km return) detour to the right would bring you to Mezapos, a forlorn-looking fishing village (🍽) with a decent pebbly beach to its north; a (3km return) detour to the left would take you via Mina to Polemitas, set at the foot of Mt Sangias. Barren and forbidding though they appear, these mountain valleys conceal terraced fields and shepherds' huts.

The main tour continues south for 3km, then turns right (30km; signed to the Tsitsiris Castle hotel in Stavri).

After 1km you could turn right for a (3km return) detour to the hamlet of Episkopi, below which lies a homonymous chapel — presumably a bishop's seat — with restored exterior and well-preserved frescoes (⛪; key with warden).

Ignoring the Episkopi turn, and keeping right through a one-way loop outside **Psio** (Ψιο), you reach a left bend and bus shelter at the edge of Stavri (33km). Turn right here, go through **Stavri** and, keeping right, drive to the foot of the hilltop hamlet of **Ayia Kyriaki** (34km). See Walk 13 on page 78 for directions to the **Odigitria Chapel** (one of my favourite picnic spots in the Mani; *P*) and **Tigani Castle**.

Then return and continue south past the bus shelter (35km), through **Payia** and **Trohalakas**. The steep-sided hill on your right is ancient Ippola (⛪), and its flat, overgrown summit is dotted with old cisterns and walls. At the junction outside **Kounos** (37.5km), keep left, go through the village centre (🍽) and, by a stone shrine, turn right to pass a grey mast on the left. From this stone-walled lane through olive

21

groves you can see the Tainaron Peninsula ahead to the left and even make out the lighthouse. At a crumbling tower (39km), turn left downhill. The valley of Pepon, shown on page 82, is visible straight ahead, with the twin towers of Leontakis standing guard on the hilltop (Walk 14). Keep right and zigzag down to the next plateau, ignoring two right turns to Ohia and a left turn in between. The narrow concrete lane descends a gully and enters **Gerolimenas** (43km ⛰✕▮; photograph page 80), where Walk 14 begins and ends, through the 'back door'. Keep left across the dry gully and, at an oblique junction, turn right along the seafront. After a right bend, turn left towards ALIKA and VATHIA, and keep right at the main road. Beware cows using the warm afternoon road as a bed!

In **Alika** (46km), at a 5-way junction, keep right (straight on) towards VATHIA. After a dangerous 90° left bend, you pass the signposted ancient site of **Kainipolis** on the right (47km **Π**). If you want a swim, you can walk down a small lane, past a 'no entry' sign, to a protected, pebbly cove.

The road continues past **Kiparissos** and another dangerous 90° left bend, with views back (north) to the 'bristling ridge' of Mountanistika (Walk 14, detour). You pass (lower) **Vathia**, with its new houses and two adjacent coves, and wind up to old **Vathia** (52km). This most spectacular of tower-villages warrants some exploration: there are countless towers in various states of repair (some were restored by the Greek Tourist Board as hostels, but no longer operate as such), a roofless chapel, a panoramic terrace (perfect for picnics; ***P***) and a resident barn owl. Continue on the road hugging the steep mountainside, past a wooded picnic area and down to the isthmus of Marmari. You pass a left turn to 'ΛΑΓΙΑ 8ΚΜ' (55km), which will be your onward route.

For the present keep right, to drive out to Cape Tainaron (perhaps referring to the large-scale map on page 85). Ignore a left fork to Porto Kayio. On the knoll above you is the ruined fort of **Harakas**, shown on page 84. Ahead you see the hamlet and sandy beaches of **Marmari** — good swimming, though crowded in summer.

Before you get there (56km), fork left towards '*PALIROS*', and, by some wheely bins and multiple signposts (57km), turn right for the ancient site and lighthouse of Tainaron (passing the parking bay for Walk 15). The road runs above the deep inlet of Vathy, whose sheltered, pebbly beach is accessible from Paliros on foot. It ends at the houses of **Kokkinoyia** (60km ✕▮), from where the ruins of Poseidon's sanctuary★

The tower houses of Vathia

Marmari Beach and village

and the mosaic circle are a few minutes' walk away — and the lighthouse at **Cape Tainaron** a good half hour. See Short walk 15 on page 83 for directions and further information.

Return from the cape to the ΛΑΓΙΑ signpost (65km) and turn right, then immediately left up a good dirt road (due to be asphalted 'quite soon') towards ΛΑΓΙΑ (Layia). This winds steeply uphill, with excellent views back over the isthmus (📷), to just below **Kainouria Hora** (67km), where a road joins from the left and the surface improves. Crossing a bleak plateau, you rejoin the Alika–Layia road by a shrine on a windy pass (70km).

Turn right and follow the road through the sleepy village of **Layia** (73km). The scenic road then descends (📷), past the scattered towers of **Dimaristika**, to the coast at **Kokkala** (79km ▲ ✕ ⬛). At the entrance to the village, by a left bend, a path heads right to the lovely pebbly cove and seasonal taverna of ΜΑΡΑΘΟΣ. Continue north through the straggling village and on to **Nyfi**/'Nymfi', a collection of fortified hamlets perched at intervals up the steep mountainside. After the main hamlet of **Mesa Hora**, at a right bend (84km), a right turn takes you down to the 'beach tavern' and hidden pirates' cove of ΑΛΥΠΑ (**Alypa**; *P*). There is enough shade under the cliffs for a picnic.

Continuing north, you pass below the cragtop towers of **Drimos** and **Argilia** to reach **Flomohori** (92km). Keep left in front of its church, towards Αρεοπολη, to a fork (94km).

The main tour heads right here*,

towards Κοτρωνας, Γυθειο. You pass through **Kotronas** (97km ▲ ✕ ⬛), with its seafront cafés and beach, and continue round the bay, following signs to SKOUTARI and GYTHIO. Suddenly the road improves, carving a wide, straight swathe along the mountainside. After crossing a coastal plain (108km), ignore a right turn to the beach and climb into **Skoutari** (109km ▲ ✕ ⬛). Keep right round its one-way system, and leave the village. At the next three junctions, keep left, right and left, following signs to ΓΥΘΕΙΟ. At the main AREOPOLIS–GYTHION ROAD (115km), turn left and follow this up to the crossroads (124km) between Vachos (left) and Kelefa (right).

Turn right and, in **Kelefa** village (128km), keep left along a dirt road heading southwest. After 1km you reach ruined **Kelefa Castle**, a low rectangular wall with chunky round bastions. It was built by the Turks in the 17th century to control Itilo's spiralling slave trade, and soon afterwards fell into Venetian hands. The **Milolangado Gorge** forms a dramatic natural wall to its north, which you can see if you walk around the top of its 700m perimeter wall.

Return the same way to the main road (134km) and follow it south-west. Approaching **Areopolis**, keep left for the centre (139km).

**For a faster journey back to Areopolis, keep left, along the main road, which climbs past the hamlets of Loukadika* and Himara, crosses a saddle between two barren mountains and reaches Areopolis in 11km (105km).

Car tour 4: LEONIDION, MT PARNON AND THE ARCADIAN COAST

Leonidion • Kosmas • Geraki • Polydroso • (Malevis Nunnery) • Astros • Paralia Tirou • Leonidion

197km/122mi; 4-5h driving time
Walks en route: 20, 21, 22, 23, (24, 25)
Opening times
Geraki: best in the morning or late afternoon (the warden does not keep official opening times)
Monasteries: only visitable in the morning or late afternoon

Picnic suggestions: medieval site of **Geraki** (50km), cave-chapel of **Ayios Ioannis** (from Polydroso, 87km — a 30min hike each way); **EOS refuge** (3km return detour from the junction at 105km)

If you want to get well and truly off the beaten track, this tour explores some of the Peloponnese's remotest villages, its most rugged coastline and its largest swathes of fir forest. That's not to say it is completely culture free: there are two functioning monasteries en route (and several more just off it), a ruined Frankish hilltown, and the last remaining pockets of Tsakonian culture and language (see box on page 104). Describing a circuit around the high summits of Mt Parnon, which form the spine of the eastern finger, the only sizeable settlement en route is the delightful, cliff-ringed market town of Leonidion, which I have chosen as the start- and end-point. There are several places to stay on the coast nearby at Plaka and Poulithra. You could probably manage the 200km or so in a day, but if you want to stop en route and do some walking or further exploration, the old school of Polydroso has been converted to a simple guesthouse, while Kosmas, Ayios Petros and several of the coastal villages have a choice of hotels and pensions. If you are driving to or from Athens, try and work at least one half of this circuit into your journey.

Follow the old main road west through the bottleneck centre of **Leonidion** (🏨✕🚗🅿), or take the bypass road which runs next to the dry riverbed and rejoins the old main road at the edge of town. You pass the right turn to 'Βασκινα 14'. Look up to the high cliffs on your left, to spot the shining white stain of the monastery of **Ayios Nikolaos** (also called **Sintzas Monastery**), apparently hanging just below the rim of the gorge (photograph page 109). Walk 23 passes the monastery, but you can get a similar experience elsewhere, a short way along this tour. The dry gorge opens out briefly at a river

junction, where the road bears up the right-hand valley and the cliff walls close in again. Ahead of you another clutch of white buildings hangs off an orange-grey cliff. To get there, ignore the right turn (12km) to 'Palaiochori 9' etc, and curl uphill to the signed turning to **Panayia Elona★** (or Elonis; 15km). It is definitely worth the short drive and 5-minute walk into this religious sanctuary, now home to a handful of nuns, who will show you into the chapel to admire the miraculous icon carved by St Luke.

Then continue up the main road to the village of **Kosmas** (29km), where the road deposits you in the

The cliff-ringed cemetery at Leonidion

shady central square. Take a breath of fresh mountain air — and, why not, a sip of fresh mountain tea at one of the two cafés here — before continuing over the beautiful wooded pass (1200m; 🖼) towards GYTHION etc. The rugged ridge of **Mt Parnon** stretches north, and southwards dwindles in a series of lower peaks to the sea near Monemvasia. Descending into Laconia, the scenery becomes more arid and monotonous, with a few corrugated iron goatsheds breaking up the shrub-specked earth.

At 44km, at a junction, turn left towards GERAKI. Keep left to drive through the modern town centre of **Geraki** (46km) — slowly, to make sure you are spotted. This should ensure, thanks to a modern equivalent of the bush telephone, that the warden catches you up on your way to the site, if he is not there already. Getting there involves two more left turns and a sinuous ascent to the gate of the medieval town★ (50km ⛪👣*P*). From here you must continue on foot: take sturdy footwear, some water and, if you want, a picnic. The warden may accompany you to the 13th-century castle and basilica at the top, unlocking a couple of Byzantine chapels en route. A tip is expected (unless entrance fees have since been introduced). If you can't find the warden, try calling him on (27320) 71393 or 71208.

Return to the junction west of Geraki town (57km) and continue straight over, heading west towards AYII ANARGYRI and GORITSA. After 1.5km, turn right towards KALLITHEA. Continue through **Kallithea** (71km) and up into the intermittent stands of fir, ignoring a left turn to Agriani. The road crosses another 1200m pass, with the barren flanks of

Psari Rahi (Fish Ridge) to your right. From the pass descend to a junction (87km) — with a blue signpost, shrine and a spring beneath a boulder. To your left lies the perfectly enclosed village of **Polydroso**, or Tzitzina, as it is called locally. Regularly snow-bound in winter, but coming alive in summer thanks to its cool mountain climate, it makes a great walking base (see Walk 21). If nothing else, do try and hike up to the cave-chapel of Ayios Ioannis (*P*). It's a divine place, with a series of ladders climbing inside the rock to a wonderful look-out or picnic spot. The path (20-30min each way) climbs steeply to the right from a point 200m south of this junction; keep left after 7min (map pages 104-105). Continuing northwest, you pass another left turn to the village centre (88km), and then fork right (91km) towards VAMVAKOU etc. At the T-junction in the fir-clad valley of **Plati Potami** (Broad River; 96km), turn right towards the Καταφυγιο ΕΟΣ (EOS refuge) etc. Ignore three subsequent right turns; although they lead through some splendid, forested scenery, they are unsurfaced and bumpy in places. The first of these turns comes at the watershed (100km) and is signed to 'Kosmas 38'; when it is eventually surfaced, it will make a lovely return route to Leonidion via Paleohori. The next is signed to 'Prastos 18, Ag Vasilios 20', and the third to 'Kastanitsa 12, Sitaina 17'. This is also due to be asphalted 'soon', and will make another possible return route — via the Vrasiatis Gorge and Ayios Andreas. But you should always keep left, following the signs to Καταφυγιο. Finally you reach a junction (105km), where a left turn would take you to the Katafigio EOS refuge after just 1.5km; it's a panoramic place for a picnic (☞*P*; Walk 20), but there is no water. The main tour keeps right here, crossing the path to the bald summit of Mt Parnon (Walk 20) by a wooden sign on the left, 'KPONION 3H' and red square waymark (106km). Continue downhill, ignoring dirt roads to the left (107.5km, 108.5km) and the right (108.5km; this leads in 5.3km to the alternative pick-up point for Walk 20, near the Malavazo summit — look out for two wooden signposts).

When you reach a junction (118km), where the busy village of Ayios Petros (✗🍴🏠🅿) is 3km to your left, turn right towards MALEVIS NUNNERY, below which you soon pass (122km). It's a huge, whitewashed building looking more like a holiday resort than a monastery, well-attended by silent but welcoming nuns (see page 102). Follow the small, surfaced road down through the dry plateau of **Xirokambos**, a featureless semi-desert in summer, awash with yellow flowers in spring. Keep right to pass above the villages of **Ayios Ioannis** (131km ⛪🎋) and **Orini Meligou** (134km), both deserted in winter. The former, if you turn left into the centre (signed 'To Neromyli'), has a lovely church, huge plane tree and stone-built picnic tables. Ignore a right turn to Haradros and Platanos (137km), pass a crossroads to the village of Elliniko and wind down to the modern, charmless town of **Astros** (148km 🅿✗🍴). Bear right through the southern quarters of

town, called 'Heimerini Meligou' ('Winter' Meligos, as opposed to the 'summer' or mountain Meligos you passed earlier).

At the MAIN ROAD (149km) turn right, with the flat, mosquito-ridden coast at **Paralio Astros** (🏠🛏✗🅿🍴) to your left, and the Frankish castle just visible above the town. Keep straight through **Ayios Andreas** (175km ✗🅿⊕🍴) — pausing only to buy some of its famous peaches — and past the bizarre resort-town of **Arkadiko Horio** (162km), built by Greeks returning from the US for their retirement or holidays. The road wiggles past the wonderful headlands and olive-covered bays of the Arcadian coast — **Krioneri** and **Zaritsi** make good swimming spots — to the bay of Tiros and Sapounakeïka — **Paralia Tirou** (or Paralia Tirosapounakeïkon, if you want a tongue-twister; 177km 🛏✗🅿🍴). You can drop into town and along the rather blandly developed beachfront for some fresh whitebait before rejoining the main road further south (178km).

The last stretch of road is one of the most scenic of all, winding high above enticing, turquoise beaches, and dotted with tastefully-restored German holiday homes. You pass the right turn to Melana (184km) and a left turn (186km) to the fishing village of Livadi, both of which feature in Walk 22. Rounding a corner above the drab beach village of **Sambatiki**, the cliffs and coast of Leonidion and Poulithra stretch before you, glowing lilac in the evening light. The road hugs the base of the rockface, turning inland to pass below some ruined windmills and into **Leonidion** (197km).

Car tour 5: MONEMVASIA AND THE VATIKA PENINSULA

Monemvasia • Elliniko • Neapoli • (Kastania) • (Velanidia) • (Ayia Marina Chapel) • Neapoli • (Elafonisos) • (Panaritis Beach) • (Archangelos Beach) • Elika • Monemvasia

96km/60mi; 3h driving time, plus up to 130km/81mi; 4h of detours. In a day you could manage one or two detours and still have time for a swim. If you want to try some of the walks, or cross to the idyllic beaches of southern Elafonisos, you'll probably need to stay over — in Neapoli (choice of hotels), *Velandia (simple rooms),* or *Elafonisos (choice of pensions).*
Walks en route: 26, (27-30)
Picnic suggestions: Paradisi (23km on the 'Mountain villages' detour), cave chapel of **Ayios Ioannis** (14km on the Velanidia detour; 30min return on foot)

The wonderfully preserved Byzantine town of Monemvasia, sitting on its vast sea-washed rock (photograph page 121), is the furthest most travellers reach down the eastern finger of the Peloponnese. But there's a lot more to the peninsula than that. Continuing past sandy beaches and the sleepy island of Elafonisos, you reach the harbour town of Neapoli, set beneath imposing mountains. This is the beginning of the Vatika, a little-visited region of picturesque mountain villages, hidden pirates' coves and cliffside monasteries. The limited road network and the steep, rocky terrain make a circular drive impossible, but my suggested detours from Neapoli offer, with a minimum of route-retracing, a fascinating insight into a region that escaped the guidebooks.

From the landward end of the causeway in **Monemvasia★** (♛♁♠✕♟M♞) follow signposts south towards NOMIA, NEAPOLI 43 etc. Ahead of you lies the barren, rocky east coast. Beyond a petrol station, head inland to a heavily signposted junction (4km), where you keep right. The road climbs past a left turn to Nomia, through terraced hillsides with olive and cypress trees, before levelling out beneath a pine grove (11km ♒). Just after the hamlet of **Lira** (13km), follow the main road left, climbing through heathland and garrigue, with wonderful views (☞) over the western seaboard. Keep an eye out for eagles. After passing through **Elliniko** (18km ✕♞) ignore the left turn to Foutia. At 22km, cut left down a concrete road signed ΚΡΥΟ– ΒΡΥΣΗ — ΝΕΑΠΟΛΗ, to reach the main road (25km), where you turn left towards NEAPOLI. You may spot the chapel of **Ayii Anargyri** built into the rock face of a low hill on your right. Ignore a left turn to a quarry and, in **Ayii Apostoli** (33km ♞), ignore a right turn to Elafonisos. Keep along the eucalyptus-lined main road, observing the speed limits carefully (speed trap territory). At the entrance to **Neapoli** (38km ✕♠♞♞) fork right towards the Παραλια (seafront) and continue for 1km (39km). Before taking any of the detours recommended overleaf, you may want to stop at one of the seafront cafés or stalls for a coffee and a sticky cake, or an ouzo and some grilled octopus. The easy return to Monemvasia follows the main road north, past **Elika** (42km ♞♞), to the junction with the MOLAI–MONEMVASIA ROAD (47km), where you turn right to **Monemvasia** (96km). On the way, detours lead to three superb beaches (see page 29).

27

Detours from Neapoli

1 Mountain villages circuit (*27-31km return*) — a fascinating glimpse of 'the other side of the mountain'. From the seafront, turn left between the Royal Restaurant and Hotel Aïvali. Then follow the road inland, straight over a crossroads, towards MESOHORI. You may spot a ruined castle on a hilltop to your left, which is best visited by turning left towards ΑΓ ΠΑΡΑΣΚΕΥΗ on a concrete lane (4km) and referring to page 122 (Walk 27; large-scale map page 124). Otherwise, continue up the winding road, with a bird's-eye view over Neapoli. Ignore the left turn into Mesohori (7km), but take the right turn into **Faraklo** 1.5km further on. The Panorama Café is usually open, and lives up to its name (☕☺📷).

Continuing uphill, the road zigzags up to the 500m pass below Mt Profitis Ilias (744m), which can be cloud-covered even in summer. You then descend through wild, scrub-covered hills, with glimpses north as far as Monemvasia, to a junction (13km). Ignore the left turn to Ano Kastania ('upper chestnut village'), and follow the unsurfaced road right, enjoying views (📷) over Kato Kastania, to the next junction (16km). If the cave of **Ayios Andreas** (∩) has finally been opened to the public (which I doubt), it promises to be worth the 2km detour to the left at this point (large-scale map page 127). If you continue 2km past the cave you reach the sheltered bay of **Kamili**, which has a small beach, several holiday huts (the Greek equivalent of a caravan site), and a chapel with shady yard and water tap.

To continue the circuit, turn right into **Kato Kastania** (signed as 'KASTANEA'; 18km 🍴). The village has a remote, mountainous feel,

with a single café serving a single-figure population (see Walk 28 on page 126). The steep concrete road improves as soon as you leave the village and shortly gains an asphalt surface (due to be extended to the cave in 2003). To the left are the craggy summits of **Mt Vavila**, and you soon cross the saddle (📷), ignoring a left turn to Ayia Katerini chapel. Neapoli and its hinterland are spread before you like a tablecloth, with the sea and Mani Peninsula behind. Walk 27 traverses the lower flanks of Vavila to cross the road at this point, en route for Faraklo (large-scale map page 124).

Continue down to **Paradisi** village (23km *P*), passing its thickly-shaded church on the left (tap, plastic tables and chairs; possible picnic spot) and its crumbling houses and watermills on your right. Sadly, the marked walk (Δ1 waymarks) from here to Neapoli is very overgrown. At 25km you reach a T-junction outside Kalenia, with Neapoli 2km to your right.

2 Velanidia (*28-31km return*) — — the region's most beautiful village and best base for walks; photograph page 6. Follow the main road south from Neapoli. Almost immediately after the Kalenia junction (2km) fork right, to pass around the village of **Lachi**. After 2.5km, at a junction in the middle of nowhere (4.5km), turn left and wind your way up the heather-covered hills to the pass of **Vavila** (500m; Walk 27). The other side of this mountain, Krithina (794m), is even more spectacular than Profitis Ilias, with giddy views down to the coast and up to the summit crags. At a right hairpin bend (12.5km), a concrete road forks left to the cove of **Ayios Pavlos**, one of the loveliest in the Vatika. Getting there involves 4km of dirt track and a short walk (see page 126 and map page 127). Continuing round the bend, you are suddenly confronted with the wonderful façade of **Velanidia** village (☎): close-packed, red-tiled houses smiling at you with balcony-mouths and shutter-eyes, all hemmed round by terraced olive groves and russet cliffs. Park at the top of the village (14km), leaving space for the bus to turn. Then walk down to the centre (⬥✕🍴), or up to the **cave-chapel of Ayios Ioannis** (15min; *P*): follow the concrete lane uphill for five minutes, then turn right up some steps. The chapel makes a cool picnic spot, though there is no water or seating.

If you fancy a swim, the narrow road does continue steeply down through Velanidia, keeping left (signed Παραλια or BEACH) to its tiny fishing harbour and grey-sand beach (3km return). If you prefer a short, flattish stroll, follow Walk 29 as far as Panayia Dekapentistra or the ruined windmill and back (1h-1h20min; map pages 130-131). Drive back the same way.

3 Ayia Marina (*33km return*). For the details on the petrified forest, sunken city and the hike to Ayia Irini Monastery★, see pages 130-131 (Walk 30). Follow Detour 2 above as far as the 'junction in the middle of nowhere' (4.5km). Then continue south through the size-able village of **Ayios Nikolaos** (7km ✕🍴), following signs for Profitis Ilias (a fishing hamlet, *not* the mountain of the same name). Ignore the right turn to Korakas and Limni (11km) and keep straight on along the (now unsurfaced) road. Fork left for Ayia Marina (12km), and go straight over the intersection (14km). At a T-junction (15km), turn sharp left over a rocky ledge, and park beside the small chapel of **Ayia Marina**. Return the same way.

Beach detours

On the return leg to Monemvasia, three fine swimming places lie between 2-12km off your route.

1 Simos Beach on Elafonisos (*14km + 11km ⛴ return*). From **Ayii Apostoli** (🚌) turn left towards Elafonisos (*n.b. there is no signpost at the turning itself, which is shortly before a BP station*). In **Ayios Georgios** (3km 🚌), bear slightly right, following signs to MEGALI SPILIA etc. At **Megali Spilia** (4km 🚌), bear left along the main road and through **Viglafia** (6km ⛺✕🍴). 0.5km after Viglafia, there is a left turn to Paralia Pountas, a sandbank beyond the Strongyli Lagoon which offers good swimming and bird-watching (herons, egrets). Keeping right after Viglafia brings you to the tiny landing stage of **Pounta** (7km), from where car ferries and passenger launches cross to **Elafonisos** (timetable page 134). This low island swarms with campers in summer, and offers seaside solitude in spring and autumn. From Elafonisos port follow the road south, past **Lefki (Sarakiniko) Bay** (4km), to the idyllic sands of **Simos Beach** (5.5km), the island's loveliest bathing spot. Junipers — a rare local subspecies called 'cedars' in most guidebooks — offer shade and wind-shelter. If time permits, leave your car at Pounta, cross in the passenger launch, and walk to Simos and back (1h20min each way).

2 Panaritis Beach (*8km return*). In **Elika**, turn left to MARATHIAS, LIMNES, PANARITIS, and at the coast (2.5km) keep right to **Panaritis Beach** (4km).

3 Archangelos Beach (*4km return*). 4km north of **Elika**, turn sharp left ('ARHAGELOS') to reach this attractive little fishing village (2km ⛺✕🍴), with its sandy beach and — in summer — buzzing cafés.

29

Walking

As anyone who has ever walked in Greece will know, getting off the beaten track can bring you inspiring and infuriating moments in equal measure. Wild flowers and herbs, cobbled *kalderimia*, shady forests, glorious views, smiling shepherds, remote chapels, warm sunshine and cool spring water provide some of the inspiration. The correspondingly infuriating experiences are prickly bushes, new dirt roads, forest fires, cloud cover (yes, even in Greece), empty shepherds' huts, locked chapels, sunstroke and running out of water! I hope this section will help you avoid the latter and enjoy the former.

The walks

With so many forest and farm roads being bulldozed through the mountainsides, and so few people using the old trail network, you might think hiking was a thing of the past. But, happily latching on to the latest trends in tourism, a few municipalities have started re-opening and waymarking old paths, and providing accurate maps for the walker. The regions around Kardamyli, Mystras and Neapoli are cases in point, and the Leonidion area may soon follow. Whether they will be maintained or not is a moot point. But the best way to encourage it is to use the paths, keep them clear, and point out any problems to hoteliers or, better still, the authorities.

This book offers 30 walks ranging from 2km (1 hour) to nearly 20km (7 hours). All have been graded from easy to strenuous, so you know what you're letting yourself in for. Carefully researched and updated hiking maps — a rarity in Greece — accompany each walk (see key on page 34). About half of the walks are circular. The other half are linear, with advice on getting public transport or taxis back, or

solutions for turning it into a circuit if you prefer. See page 7 for details on getting about, and page 35 for suggestions on where to base yourselves.

The majority of the walks follow accepted 'trails', such as those developed by the local municipality; these are often interspersed with forest or farm tracks. A few routes cross open, pathless hillsides, where route-finding can be tricky, and experience and good observation is useful.

The land and people

On the whole, land around villages belongs to private individuals or the community, wooded land belongs to the forestry commission, and mountainsides belong to the municipality, with grazing rights allocated to shepherds.

It is surprising how often, when you think you are miles from the nearest person, you look round and see a shepherd observing you from on top of a rock, or under a shady tree. On the other hand, when you come to a village, you may be surprised to find it deserted. Many smaller mountain settlements lie empty in winter, while in summer everyone stays indoors, especially during siesta hours (14.30-17.00).

If you do meet someone, don't count on useful advice, even if you speak Greek: most are unfamiliar with maps, and out of concern for your safety will direct you to the nearest road or village, regardless of what you ask.

The notion of **public right of way** is a vague one in Greece, where population density is low and, on the whole, folk are just pleased to see foreigners exploring their area. However, it is important to note that a few of these walks cross small areas of private land which, while this is unlikely, you should be prepared to circumnavigate if asked. In my experience of walking in rural Greece, both alone and with groups, we have always been welcome, so long as we observe some obvious do's and don't's.

Do:
- Stick to the route described
- Leave gates as you find them
- Learn a few words of Greek (see page 36)
- Greet people you meet
- Dress respectfully: long sleeves/skirts in churches and monasteries; and, for your own sake, nothing too revealing at any time

Don't:
- Light fires
- Drop lit cigarettes
- Take photographs of people or church interiors without asking permission
- Leave rubbish (even where locals seem quite happy to pile their own)
- Pick wild flowers
- Swim or sunbathe topless or naked (except where it is clearly allowed)
- Take undue risks

Walk wisely

As in any country, it is important to be prepared, sensible and well-equipped when walking. These walks cross remote and rocky countryside, often miles from a telephone or surfaced road.

The most common problems are *dehydration and sunstroke.* Here's how to avoid them:

Carry plenty of water — at least 1 litre per person, even for short walks, and 2 litres per person for long walks in the summer. Check where to find springs or taps before you leave; although there is piped, drinkable water to almost every habitation, some hamlets marked on maps are no longer inhabited, or may be empty when you pass through. Spring and tap water is drinkable, but you should avoid surface water, especially downstream from livestock and human habitation. If you are running out of water, stop in the shade and cool off for a moment before drinking — that way it won't pour out as sweat quite so quickly. Try and keep your water cool — although it is handy to have it accessible (eg in a side pocket or waterbag), it is less effective when warm.

Wear a hat when it is sunny: even though it feels hotter, keeping your brain in the shade is the next most important thing to keeping well hydrated.

Wear sunscreen, especially on your nose, ears, neck, arms and (if wearing shorts) the knees and backs of your legs.

Wear sunglasses, preferably with good UV-filtering lenses, and ideally (for high altitude walks) side-pieces. If you ordinarily wear glasses, consider buying prescription sunglasses or light-reactive spectacles as an alternative to clip-on shades, which can cause annoying internal reflection.

Stop in the shade and cool off periodically. If you overheat, the best way to cool down is to place wet clothes on your forehead and wrists and sip cold water. Many walkers wet their hat every time they pass a spring. If there's no shade en route (eg Walk 17), carry 50% more water. Or you might consider carrying a parasol or umbrella, as shepherds sometimes do. Best of all, **come in spring or autumn**, or, if you have to come in summer, start really early, as the Greeks do. (See also 'Weather' opposite.)

Tortoise puzzling out one of the 'Japanese flag' waymarks seen on some of the walks

Another common problem is *route-finding*. In theory I've got lost so that you don't have to; but new roads, overgrown paths, low cloud, featureless terrain, different walking speeds and subjective terminology can scupper that theory.

Never walk alone — four is an ideal number: sociable, manageable and you fit into one taxi.

Take a compass on the remoter walks, and make sure you know how to use it.

Keep looking ahead and around for waymarks, traces of your onward path, landmarks etc.

Carry food (fruit, energy bars or a picnic) in case it ends up taking longer than you think.

Get a good map of the area — while our touring map and mini hiking maps cover the walks themselves, it is often useful to have a bigger picture (see 'Maps' on page 34).

Equipment

In addition to the above, you should always have:

A comfortable rucksack or good-sized daypack — it is better to have space left over than to walk with a jacket tied round your waist and water-bottle in your hand.

Comfortable, worn-in boots or (for the easy walks) walking shoes. Never wear brand new footwear on a long walk.

Comfortable socks — I wear thick socks even in summer; you can wash them overnight and they'll be dry in the morning.

A first aid kit, which I suggest should include painkillers, antiseptic cream or wipes, plaster or band-aids, antihistamine (for bites or stings), blister kit (padded or shaped plaster such as Compeed), safety pins, spare shoelace, whistle, tweezers, scissors and perhaps a triangular bandage.

A jacket or pullover in case of changing weather, missed return bus, etc (except perhaps on short, circular walks in settled summer weather).

And the following are recommended:

Long trousers and sleeves: against thorny undergrowth and sunburn, as well as being more acceptable in religious buildings and remote villages.

A torch: for seeing inside dark chapels and caves, or in case you are benighted.

A stick (or two): for rocky terrain, especially in gorges — even if you are not used to walking with one.

Plastic sandals or flip-flops: for getting in and out of the sea where it is rocky.

A small towel: for drying your feet after a swim; or for mopping your brow! Wet feet can lead to athlete's foot and similar infections (foot powder helps avoid this).

Small change if you plan to visit a chapel (for donations).

Mobile phone coverage is good in rural Greece, and I recommend taking a cellphone (even if used only for outgoing, emergency calls), but remember that there is rarely a signal in gorges or near the boundary between two *nomos* (counties).

If you do have an **accident**, there is *no organised mountain rescue service*. As a first resort, call your hotel or a taxi (see page 134). Otherwise, **emergency numbers** are 100 (police), 166 (ambulance) and 112 (general).

Nuisances

At some point you will come across **dogs** — guarding a flock, a hut or even roaming stray. The stray ones are rarely aggressive, and may tag along behind you in the hope of getting food (if you feed them, be prepared for a long-term relationship!). The guard dogs are usually tied up, and rarely have a bite to match their bark. Often they are just hungry, thirsty or frustrated. The sheepdogs may be untied, and may approach you, barking loudly. Stay calm and walk purposefully around the flock, *never* presenting your back to them. If there is a shepherd around, greet him loudly to alert him to your presence. And, if the dog does come towards you, and you have no stick, pick up a stone, or even an imaginary stone, and (only if necessary) throw it so it lands in front of the dog. Easy as it is to say, *never turn and run*. If dogs worry you, you could invest in an ultrasonic dog deterrent — a 'Dog Dazer'. These are widely available on the internet.

Bees are another potential nuisance. While the law forbids hives within 50m of a thoroughfare, it is no surprise that it is often flouted. If you want to pass occupied hives, cover your body and your hair (especially if you have washed it that day) as fully as possible, and walk silently past them in single file.

Two beasts you are less likely to see, but which do exist in small numbers, are **snakes** and **scorpions**. Of the former, the vast majority are harmless to humans; the only seriously venomous one is the horn-nosed viper, which is typically 60cm/2ft long, with a V-shaped line down its brown or grey back, and a pronounced triangular head with (if you get this close!) oval pupils. Watch out for sluggish snakes in long grass during springtime (tread loudly), and never assume a snake is dead. Scorpions, meanwhile, live under stones and in stone walls, so take care when climbing over one, and try to keep your children from poking fingers into dark crannies. Their sting is very painful indeed, but not the killer that some stories make out. And don't get things out of proportion — in ten years of constant hiking here, I have seen two vipers and maybe a dozen scorpions.

Finally, where there is livestock, you may come across **horseflies** (very persistent but not very painful) and occasionally **ticks** (barely noticeable but potentially awkward, so don't be shy to check each other — when swimming, for example!).

Weather

Most of these walks are best in spring and autumn, when it is cooler, quieter and more colourful. Spring (April, May) has the added advantage of wild flowers, flowing streams and a snow-capped backdrop, not to mention Greek Easter, the biggest festival in the Orthodox calendar. Autumn (late September, October) offers warmer swimming, cool winds and clear air. Winter (November to March) can also offer bright clear weather, though the days are shorter, rain is more likely, and some hotels, restaurants and public transport services shut down. Snow is common over 1500m altitude during these

months, and at night or in cloud it will ice over. Summer (June to mid-September) is really too hot for comfortable walking, as well as being more crowded and expensive; but you can get away with it if you start early and/or choose the high-altitude walks (17, 20, 21). Most television channels broadcast a short, pictorial weather report after the news, typically around 21.30.

Maps

When the first edition of this book was written, **Road Editions** kindly let us adapt their maps as the basis for our walking maps. This was the best cartography available at the time — both for touring (scale 1:125,000 for Messinia and Laconia, 1:250,000 for the entire Peloponnese) or hiking (1:50,000). As helpful as they were, they only showed a selection of paths and even those not always accurately.

But in recent years, some excellent large-scale maps have become commercially available.

Atrapos (telephone/fax: +30 210 6718559, atrapos@in.gr) produce an excellent 1:25,000 hiking map of the Vatika Peninsula (contours every 20m), with a 1:50,000 touring map on the reverse. It is, unfortunately, hard to find — I got mine from the *dhemos Vion* (municipality in Neapoli), who helped to produce it. There is a similar map of Kynouria (Leonidion and Mt Parnon).

Anavasi (telephone/fax: +30 210 3210152, www.anavasi.gr) produce excellent 1:25,000 'local' maps covering different areas of

the Peloponnese (contours every 20m), as well as wider-ranging but less detailed 1:50,000 maps. Serious cartophiles can try to get to grips online with the **Hellenic Military Geographical Service** (http://web.gys.gr), on which all of the above are based. These Greek Army maps are available from an E-shop or may be collected in Athens (to get them, you must fill out a request form from the above website, then go to their headquarters: 'HAGS' or 'ΤΥΣ', 4 Evelpidon St; Tel: 30 210 8206662).

But we hope you will find the maps in this book amply detailed for all the walks you undertake. You should be able to trace the routes in advance on the web — either using Google Earth or your preferred map source.

Below is a key to the symbols used on the walking maps.

══════	main road
─────	secondary road
≡≡≡≡≡	minor road or motorable track
───────	rough/jeep track
- - - - -	path or trail
2 →	main walk
2 →	alternative route
— 400 —	height in metres
●▸	spring, tap, waterfall, etc
♁♁	church or monastery.chapel
†	shrine or cross
⊞	cemetery
⊼	picnic tables
▱	best views
⛟	bus stop
⚘	car parking
▮▮	castle, fort.tower
■	specified building
⊡	watchtower
∩∩	cave.aqueduct
⚒ ✺	quarry, mine.mill
▯	stadium
△	campsite
⛊	map continuation
⋔	ancient site

Suggested bases for walking

If you have not yet chosen your accommodation, and you want to be ideally placed for walking, the best bases are as follows:

Western finger: Pylos

Central finger
— *western foothills and coast:* Kardamyli or Stoupa
— *eastern foothills and gorges:* Mystras or Anavriti
— *Mani:* Areopolis, Stavri or Gerolimenas

Eastern finger
— *Arcadian coast:* Leonidion
— *Mt Parnon:* Polydroso
— *Vatika:* Velanidia/Neapoli

Explanatory notes

Timings are based on a steady pace with occasional pauses to catch your breath or take a photo, but excluding longer stops to drink water, identify flowers, go swimming, explore a chapel etc.

Detours are not included in the timings, but are shown separately. Always allow at least 25% on top of the walking time for rest stops, route-finding etc.

I reckon on a pace of 2-3km/h on paths, and about 4km/h on tracks and roads. Where there is a long, steady ascent, a more accurate guide is 300 metres altitude gain per hour.

The grading words **easy, fairly easy, moderate, strenuous** are, of course, *relative to each other,* and not necessarily how you yourself would rate them.

I have tried to be consistent in using the following terminology:

track: a small, unsurfaced road just passable in a vehicle (a jeep track is only passable in a high clearance vehicle)

lane: a narrow, surfaced road

trail: a wide or well-trodden footpath (except goats' trail, which means a rough, narrow route for animals)

mulepath (*kalderimi*)**:** a stone-cobbled path (sometimes overgrown)

gully: a small, usually dry valley

gorge or ravine: a deep, steep-sided valley

saddle or pass: a low point on a ridge or watershed

peak or summit: respectively, a pointy or a rounded high point

to contour: to pass round without changing altitude

to traverse: to pass round while slowly climbing or descending

waymark: a paint spot or an arrow to show the way

cairn: a small pile of stones

trig point: a low concrete column on a prominent point, used for triangulation (map-making)

shrine: a sacred box (usually on legs), or recess in a wall

A note about churches

Wherever you go in Greece, you will come across country churches, which may have been built on ancient sacred spots, or as a votive offering for a miracle or safe passage. They are rarely used today, except on the feast day of the saint to whom they are dedicated, and occasionally for a baptism or marriage, when a sizeable crowd will gather for the liturgy service. However, a candle is often kept alight — that's candle oil, not beer or ouzo, in the bottle by every chapel door! — and if you feel so moved you are welcome to make a small donation and light a candle to accompany your own wish or prayer. Make sure that it is firmly planted, so that you do not set fire to anything!

Out of respect for Orthodox tradition, you should refrain from going behind the *iconostasis* or *templon* (the rood screen, usually triple-arched, which hides the altar or *bema*). Don't take photos of icons or frescoes unless you are sure it is acceptable. If you have company, or may soon have, please cover your shoulders and legs; in some monasteries women are requested to wear skirts rather than trousers 'to avoid temptation' — though, paradoxically, a mini-skirt is fine and baggy slacks are not!

You'll find an increasing number of chapels locked — the result, apparently, of the theft of sacred relics and artwork, although I think there's also a certain amount of scare-mongering taking place. The key may be held locally; see box on page 21. I have tried to indicate this, where possible, but unfortunately the situation changes regularly.

Glossary

The most important thing when speaking Greek is to get the correct stress or emphasis. I've indicated this below with an accent above the vowel. (See the Index or the maps for accents on **place names**.) Unstressed syllables can be swallowed almost completely.

Greetings and general

Yásas! (Yásu!): Hello/Goodbye/ Cheers! (bracketed version is singular, ie when talking to one child, or one friend)

Kaliméra: Good morning

Kalispéra: Good afternoon or evening

Kaliníhta: Good night

Ti kánete? (Ti kánees?): How are you? (bracketed form is sin-gular). NB: this also means 'what are you doing?'

Ápo poo eéste?: Where are you from?

(Eémaste) apo teen Anglía/ Amerikí/Áfstralía: (We are) from England/America/Australia

Sas arésee ee Ellátha?: Do you like Greece?

Né/Óhee: Yes/No (raised eyebrows mean 'no')

Pollée oréa: Very beautiful (you can also use this for food, a room, etc)

Hárika: 'I enjoyed', ie 'It was nice talking to you.'

Kaló thrómo: 'Good road', ie 'Have a pleasant walk/drive.'

(Na páte) sto kaló: (May you go) towards the good (ie, 'farewell')

Parakaló: Please. Also used to get attention, and to say 'You're welcome'.

Efhareestó: Thank you.

Taxis

Mas paté sto Paróri?: Will you take us to Parori?

Elate na mas parté apo Kalivia stis … Come and get us from Kalivia at … (show the time on your watch)

Walking/touring

Kánoume pezoporía: We are walking (hiking)

Poo páte? Where are you going?

Páme sto Yeroliména/steen Areópoli: We are going to Gerolimenas/to Areopolis

Neró/pighí: Water/spring

(Poo eén-eh) to klithí ya teen eklisía?: (Where is) the key for the church?

(Poo eén-eh) to monopáti (ya Karthamyli): (Where is) the path (for Kardamyli)

Aristerá/Thexiá: Left/Right

Ethó/Ekée: Here/There

Tsaï (Evropaikó/Faskómilo/tou vounoú): Tea ('ordinary' tea/sage tea/mountain tea)

(Ellinikó/Nes) caffé skéto/métrio/ glikó: (Greek/instant) coffee unsugared/medium-sweet/sweet

Mé (lígho) ghála: with (a little) milk

Zestó/kaftó neró: Hot/boiling water

Na pleerósoume?: Can we pay?

Mía apótheexi: A receipt

Éhete tilekárta?: Have you got phonecards?

Boró na páro tiléfono?: May I make a phone call?

Walk 1: AROUND ANCIENT MESSENE

Distance/time: 14.9km/9.3mi; 5h15min

Grade: moderate, with 500m/1640ft total ascent/descent, mostly on dirt tracks

Equipment: water, sunhat and sunscreen, picnic. A walking stick is useful for the rocky terrain, long trousers for the prickly sections, and a jacket in case of cool winds on the mountaintop.

Opening times: Ancient Messene is open daily from 09.00-16.00, entry fee € 4. Combined entry to the site and unimpressive museum (closed Mondays) costs € 5.

Transport: 🚌 to/from Mavromati

— 30km north of Kalamata (Car tour 2) or Rizomilos (Car tour 1), following small country lanes. You'll need a good road map. 🚌 (Timetable 1) — be prepared to stay overnight.

Alternative walks

1 Ascent of Mt Ithomi (without the circuit): follow the walk up to Mt Ithomi and return to Mavromati the same way (7.8km; 3h; moderate).

2 Circuit of Mt Ithomi (without the ascent): follow the walk, omitting the ascent of Mt Ithomi (9.9km; 3h15min; very moderate

---

T he ancient site of Messene (pronounced Messíni), though somewhat off the beaten track, boasts some of Greece's best preserved classical fortifications and a ruined city still under excavation. On a mountaintop nearby are the crumbling 13th-century monastery of Voulkanou and the scant remains of a sanctuary of Zeus. This walk circles the mountain, in places following the route of the original, 9km-long city walls. For the energetic, there is also the option of climbing from the 'Laconian Gate' to the 799m summit. The mountaintop is called 'Ithomi', which means 'step', though the name is sometimes used for the whole site, just to be confusing. The walk starts and ends in Mavromati village, which lies near the ancient city centre. I suggest you visit the site which in recent years it has undergone much-needed restoration, before starting the walk.

Start the walk in **Mavromati** from what is optimistically called the *plateia* (square) — a bend in the main road 100m south of the springs which gush out of black holes (*mavro mati*: black eye). Follow the small concrete road uphill towards 'LACONIAN GATE

2KM'. As it bends sharp left, the old monastery of Voulkanou can be seen on the hilltop ahead. Just before the big CHURCH on your right (**5min**), turn right on a concrete track which descends gently. By the BREEZE-BLOCK BUILDING (**10min**), keep left,

The Byzantine monastery atop Mt Ithomi

climbing gently, now on a dirt track. At the fork (**20min**), keep left and climb steeply to the now-asphalted road (**23min**).

The onward route continues straight opposite, along a path indicated by a faint red waymark. But first, follow the road 100m to your right, to the ruined **Laconian Gate** (**25min**), the fortified entrance from the east (Sparta, Laconia). Above this gate are remains of the ancient walls crowning the already daunting rock face — you can explore these along a path opposite the SHRINE. 1km further down the road is the 'new' monastery of Voulkanou, built in the 15th century as winter quarters for the monks. Return to the point where you joined the asphalt road (**30min**) and turn right up the stony path until you reach a fork (**35min**).

Turn left here for the SUMMIT ASCENT (*or keep right if you're doing Alternative walk 2*). Pass a chunk of ancient wall and climb steeply over loose stones. At the dirt track (**45min**), turn right, uphill — ignore the short cut path opposite. When you reach some curved

limestone strata on your left (**1h**), you can pick up the path again (red spot), which curves past a MEMORIAL CROSS and rejoins the track (**1h10min**). At the end of the track (**1h22min**), continue straight past the 'no entry' sign, passing a section of the acropolis' fortification wall. 100m before the monastery, you can turn right and follow the summit-line to some TEMPLE FOUNDATIONS and the TRIG POINT atop **Mt Ithomi** (799m; **1h27min**); or continue straight on to the semi-ruined BYZANTINE MONASTERY (**1h35min**).

Although the front gate is usually locked, you can go round to the right and climb through a breach in the wall into the flower-covered yard, off which lie the (open) store-, dormitory- and dining-rooms as well as the (closed) chapel. It is built on the site of the sanctuary of Zeus Ithomatas, where in the 8th century BC, under siege by the Spartans, King Aristodemos of Messene sacrificed his daughter and had hundreds of sacrificial tripods built before finally killing himself in despair. There is a small tree at the front,

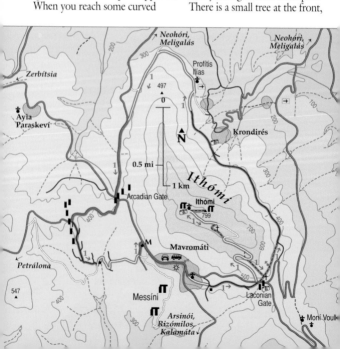

Towers and fortification walls south of the road to Petralona

with meagre shade for a picnic. The view over olive-studded fields, dense citrus orchards and splashes of white-and-red villages, is inspirational. Return the same way to the summit detour fork, or keep to the track if you prefer (**2h30min**).

TO CONTINUE THE CIRCUIT AROUND MT ITHOMI, follow the lower path (ie the right fork, when you first approached), passing a SPRING on your left (**2h35min**). Shortly after the spring, the path becomes a jeep track, descending gently. When you join a larger track (**2h45min**), keep left, descending northwards. You pass through a gate of branches and the tiny hamlet of Krondires comes into view. Above you the rocky flanks of Mt Ithomi rear up steeply — it is hard to believe that the ancient defence walls followed its ridge.

At the junction with a larger track (**3h15min**), keep left (straight on), passing the fenced, red-tiled chapel of **Profitis Ilias** (ΠΡΟΦΗΤΗΣ ΗΛΙΑΣ) on your right. Where the main track bends right and is concreted (**3h35min**), fork left on a smaller dirt track, climbing southwards. At the junction with the ASPHALT ROAD FROM NEOHORI AND MELIGALAS ('honeymilk'; **3h45min**), turn left. After 1km you reach the well-preserved **Arcadian Gate** (**4h**), through whose impregnable double portal the road, and our route, run. Turning left here would bring you to the museum and the archaeological site after 1km and back to Mavromati after 2km.

To continue the walk, turn right along the paved road towards PETRALONA for just under 1km, until you reach the best-preserved TOWERS AND FORTIFICATION WALLS (**4h15min**). There were once thirty such towers of ashlar masonry dotted along the 9km of wall. Just before the FIRST TOWER, turn left down a wide dirt track. Ignore the smaller track to the right and then two successive sharp left turns (**4h25min**). At the first right-hand bend, take a left fork down a smaller track and follow it down through a grove of young olive trees to a minor dirt track emerging from the left. Turn right and, at the next junction, with a wider track, turn left (**4h35min**). Follow this track past a farm building on your right. At the first left-hand bend ignore the smaller track heading straight on (**4h40min**). A little later, ignore the left turn — keep straight ahead. The track emerges on a minor road (**4h50min**), where a right turn leads to the site and a left takes you up to the MUSEUM and on to **Mavromati** (**5h15min**).

Walk 2: NESTOR'S PALACE • ROMANOS BEACH • PETROHORI (OR VOIDOKILIA)

Distance/time: 9km/5.6mi; 2h55min (to Petrohori)
Grade: easy, with about 200m/ 650ft descent, along dirt tracks and a sandy beach
Equipment: water, sunhat and sunscreen, picnic, swimming things, sandals for crossing streams (in spring/early summer)
Transport: 🚌 to/from Nestor's Palace (Car tour 1 at 17km). Or

🚌 from Pylos (Timetable 4). Return from Petrohori village by taxi to your car or by 🚌 to Pylos (Timetable 5)
Alternatives: Carry on to **Voido-kilia Beach** (12km/7.4mi; 4h; moderate) or **Golden Beach** (15km/9.3mi; 5h; moderate), returning by taxi or ⛴ from Golden Beach (summer only, check first).

This walk takes you from the ruined Mycenean palace of King Nestor to the sands of Romanos Beach. Gently meandering farm tracks through olive groves make it a pleasant, rather than a spectacular, walk.

Start out at **Nestor's Palace**: follow the main asphalt road downhill towards PYLOS/YIALOVA for just under 1km, to a left bend (**10min**). Here fork right on a dirt track up to a house, passing a MARBLE PLINTH (ΚΤΗΜΑ ΤΣΑΚΑΛΙ). After 50m fork left and after 80m left again, down a steep concrete track. This leaves the olive groves, descending parallel to the valley on your left, and becomes narrower. As you approach the valley floor (**25min**), keep left along a smaller track into the olive groves again, and then follow this 90° right, dropping down terraces, to the STREAMBED. This last stretch crosses private groves, and if by chance you are hailed, an

explanation that you are walking to Romanos ('páme sto Romanó me ta póthia') should prompt smiles and hand-gestures in the direction of the sea.
Cross the stream by a clump of BAMBOO (**33min**) — you may need to take your shoes off in spring or after heavy rains, when it is running — and keep left along a track, initially parallel to the stream, then bending away from it. A second track joins from the left, and you start to climb. At the T-junction of tracks (**45min**), turn left. At a CORRUGATED IRON SHED (**52min**), keep left, soon passing some BREEZE BLOCK HUTS. Where the main track bends left to cross a concrete bridge over the stream

Olive groves below Nestor's Palace

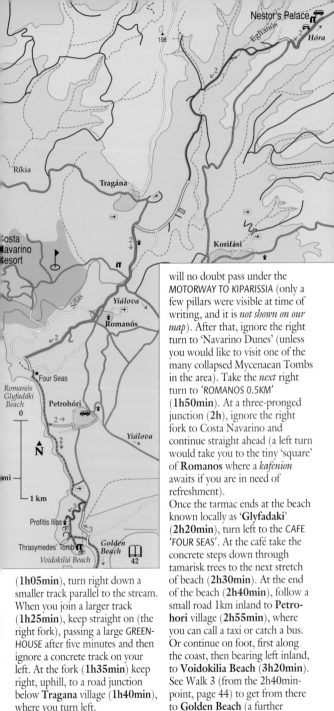

will no doubt pass under the *MOTORWAY TO KIPARISSIA* (only a few pillars were visible at time of writing, and it is *not shown on our map*). After that, ignore the right turn to 'Navarino Dunes' (unless you would like to visit one of the many collapsed Mycenaean Tombs in the area). Take the *next* right turn to 'ROMANOS 0.5KM' (**1h50min**). At a three-pronged junction (**2h**), ignore the right fork to Costa Navarino and continue straight ahead (a left turn would take you to the tiny 'square' of **Romanos** where a *kafenion* awaits if you are in need of refreshment).

Once the tarmac ends at the beach known locally as '**Glyfadaki**' (**2h20min**), turn left to the CAFE 'FOUR SEAS'. At the café take the concrete steps down through tamarisk trees to the next stretch of beach (**2h30min**). At the end of the beach (**2h40min**), follow a small road 1km inland to **Petrohori** village (**2h55min**), where you can call a taxi or catch a bus. Or continue on foot, first along the coast, then bearing left inland, to **Voidokilia Beach** (**3h20min**). See Walk 3 (from the 2h40min-point, page 44) to get from there to **Golden Beach** (a further 3km/1h).

(**1h05min**), turn right down a smaller track parallel to the stream. When you join a larger track (**1h25min**), keep straight on (the right fork), passing a large GREEN-HOUSE after five minutes and then ignore a concrete track on your left. At the fork (**1h35min**) keep right, uphill, to a road junction below **Tragana** village (**1h40min**), where you turn left.

After nearly 1km of asphalt, you

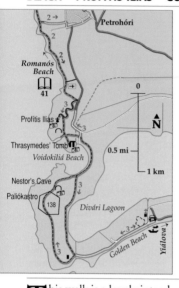

See also photo pages 10-11
Distance/time: 9km/5.6mi; 3h40min
Grade: easy; the walk is short and fairly gentle, apart from the steep descent from the castle to Nestor's Cave, for which you may need to use your hands. The terrain is mostly paths and sand.
Equipment: water, sunscreen, swimming things/towel, picnic
Transport: 🚌 to/from Golden Beach (detour on Car tour 1). Or ⛴: in summer you can catch a water-taxi from Pylos to the jetty by the car park at Golden Beach.
Short walk: Divari — Paliokastro — Nestor's Cave — Voidokilia Beach — Divari. 5.5km/3.4mi; 2h. Just do the first loop of the main walk.

This walk is a lovely introduction to the best of Pylos bay: the Frankish castle of Paliokastro, Nestor's mythical cave, the *tholos* tomb of Nestor's son Thrasymedes, and the implausibly perfect horseshoe of Voidokilia ('cow's belly') Beach. The walk describes two loops, like a figure of eight, crossing at Voidokilia Beach — so you can swim there on your way out and on your way back. This beach does get crowded in summer: ideally, go in spring/autumn, or go early in the day — or, failing that, seek out the 'secret cove' beyond the archaeological site.

Start at the CAR PARK at **Golden Beach**, reached by taking the left fork at the end of the beach road, signed 'Paleokastro'. Walk along the dirt road heading west, with the **Divari Lagoon** on your right, and on your left the long strip of Golden Beach with the Bay of Navarino behind you. You pass a track turning off right to the pump station (which maintains the lagoon's water level), and then a short, signposted nature trail on wooden walkways. Even from the dirt road you are liable to see egrets, herons, black-winged stilts, cormorants and (in season) flamingoes, while the beaches

around the lagoon are nesting sites for two endangered species, the loggerhead turtle (*Caretta caretta*) and the African chameleon — which is why you are asked to leave your car at the edge of the wetland area, and to refrain from sticking parasols deep into the sand.
After 700m (**10min**), with a fenced area ahead of you, fork left up a dirt road which crosses the canal linking lagoon and sea. After another 600m (**20min**), where the dirt road ends, cross the second canal in front of you at its seaward end. You pass a brown 'NAVARINO CASTLE' SIGN and follow the path

Paliokastro (top): the walls were built in 1278 by the Frankish prince Nicholas II of St Omer, using older foundations, and enclose an area of about 100 by 200 metres. Leaving the castle ruins involves a steep step down (below), but this can be avoided.

which climbs up left, below a round tower. To your left are the narrow straits separating Sphakteria island from the mainland. In 425 BC the Spartans found themselves trapped on the island by the Athenians, who had taken the (unfortified) hill of Paliokastro. Promising them freedom if they succeeded, the Spartans made their *helots* (slaves) fetch supplies by swimming across the straits underwater, using bamboo as snorkels. But all was in vain: the Spartans (for the first time) surrendered.

Where the path flattens slightly in open ground (**25min**), keep right towards the visible castle walls. You climb steadily through woods of juniper and tree-spurge (you may notice some old red waymarks). You are heading for the midpoint of the castle wall, where a large section has crumbled away at the base. When you reach it, keep left through the remains of a gate and into the outer enceinte of the castle, **Paliokastro** (**45min**).

Hop left up onto the perimeter wall and follow it to the right with dramatic views over the sea (but vertigo-sufferers may prefer to follow the base of the wall). Buzzards and peregrine falcons soar above the sea cliffs here. Shortly before another wall converges from your right (**55min**), clamber down the ruined steps. Go right, up to the main enceinte wall and pick your way carefully across the rock-strewn rubble, looking out for collapsed cisterns and hidden boulders. You pass a round tower base, then reach a large hole (**1h05min**) in the north wall through which you must leave the castle — it involves a steep step down (see picture above). If you don't fancy it, it is possible, from the 'ruined steps' above, to skirt the outside of the perimeter wall to just below this hole.

From here a small, steep path descends over bands of rock — you may need to use your hands from time to time. The views over the enclosed horseshoe bay of Voidokilia are the stuff of picture-postcards (see pages 10-11). A final, steep drop brings you to **Nestor's Cave** (**1h15min**) on your right — a tunnel-like entrance with a large rear chamber where Nestor kept his cattle — or Hermes hid those he had stolen from Apollo, depending on which story you read. Keeping left from the cave, continue your descent through sage bushes, then across open land and finally down a sand dune, to the left-hand end of **Voidokilia Beach** (**1h25min**), where you can plunge into the shallow, sun-warmed waters.

Coastal walk through asphodels below Paliokastro

Walk along the water's edge to your right, passing the direct path back to Golden Beach (your return route). At the far end of the bay (**1h35min**), follow the rough road heading north. After 400m, turn left across the CONCRETE BRIDGE over the canal and follow the road (now asphalted) for a further 300m — to where a dirt track forks left, next to a BLACK SIGN (**1h45min**). Turn left up this track and keep left, passing a crumbling segment of wall. Follow the track all the way up to the chapel of **Profitis Ilias** (Prophet Elijah) on the summit of the hill (**2h**). With its sheltered portico, stone bench and open views up the coast, it makes a lovely lunch spot.

From the chapel, retrace your steps for about three minutes, to where the track bends left; here turn right, past a large juniper tree, along a small path squeezing through Jerusalem sage bushes. It becomes rocky underfoot. Cross a clearing with a CAVE-SHELTER on your right. At the open field (**2h15min**), the path continues past a BROWN SIGNPOST ('Archaeological Site') at the far end. But first, head right, down a small, steep path through low junipers to a tiny, secret, FAN-SHAPED COVE (**2h20min**) which you may have

44

glimpsed on your descent — the perfect setting for a children's adventure story, or for a private swim (but beware the sharp stones and occasional sea-urchin).

Back at the SIGNPOST (**2h25min**), continue along a small path, weaving south through dense bushes, to the MYCENEAN THOLOS TOMB — supposed to be that of Thrasymedes, Nestor's son (**2h30min**). It looks more like a large, roofless, stone igloo with outlying rectangular graves or cisterns. There is a great view over Voidokilia from the far side. Return to the BROWN SIGNPOST and turn right (east), towards the lagoon, along a rocky/sandy path down to the (now familiar) northern end of Voidokilia Bay (**2h40min**). Walk back along the curving beach and, about 50m before the end, strike inland across the sand dunes — the exact route is impossible to describe or signpost, but make for the base of the left-hand cliff below Paliokastro. The path becomes clearer and runs along the edge of the lagoon — more birdwatching opportunities. You rejoin your outward route at the second canal and small CAR PARK (**3h20min**). Follow the same dirt road back to the car park and jetty at **Golden Beach** (**3h40min**).

Walk 4: TWO SHORT WALKS NEAR PYLOS

Walk a: Seasonal waterfall near Yialova (normally flows from March to June)

Distance/time: 1km/0.6mi; 30min
Grade: easy, though the path is steep in places, and in spring you need to cross stepping stones over a stream
Equipment: walking boots, insect repellent
Transport: 🚗 to/from the waterfall car park. 1km north of Yialova (Car tour 1 at 7km), and 100 metres north of the turning to the Divari Lagoon and Golden Beach, turn right, signed 'Shinolaka 3'. After 0.9km fork right down a good dirt track (small sign to 'καταρακτης/waterfall'). Soon you can make out the falls ahead. 1.7km along this track, where it bends right to go back downstream, park the car.

Walk b: Dafnorema river-gorge and aqueduct (best from July — October)

Distance/time: 2.4km/1.5mi; 1-2 hours (depending on the season)
Grade: moderate-strenuous (depending on season). This is not so much a walk as a wade (in summer) or a fully-fledged swim (in spring). Even in autumn, when it is dry, the rock-strewn streambed and the invasive undergrowth demand *agility and care*, which is why I have graded it moderate-strenuous, despite being very short. *NB: This 'walk' has not been rechecked for this edition; it was last checked in 2005.*
Equipment: boots and clothes which you don't mind getting wet and muddy. Long sleeves are essential for the undergrowth. A stick (use a sturdy branch). In spring and early summer, you will not be able to take anything else; leave towel and spare clothes in the car. In autumn you can take camera, sunscreen etc.
Transport: 🚗 to/from a quarry near the gorge. From the Gargaliani–Kalamata junction 2.5km northeast of Pylos (start of Car tour 1), fork right towards Kalamata. After 3.2km, where the road bends left to cross a bridge, fork right and park near the limestone quarry seen ahead.

If you feel like getting away from the busy seaside to some quieter walks, the cascading stream near Yialova (Walk a) is an easily accessible, totally unexpected sight. As for Walk b, I have included this mini-adventure for the benefit of the true explorers amongst you. Imagine rounding the corner of a gorge, surrounded by grey crags and inaccessible caves, to see a three-tiered, Ottoman aqueduct spanning the sheer limestone walls overhead. The only sound is stream water gurgling through deep pools, the peeps of kestrels and falcons, and the wind rustling in the oleander bushes. You could be five thousand miles away from the crowded beaches and cafés of Pylos. In fact, you are only five.

Start Walk a from the right-hand bend in the track: walk down a small track to the left, waymarked with RED ON WHITE CIRCLES. At the ORANGE GROVE (**1min**), turn left and follow the marked path steeply up through bushes speckled with cistus, garlic, sage and *serapia* flowers. At a junction of paths (**5min**), keep right (waymark), pass some overhanging rocks, and descend steeply to the STREAM (**10min**). The dense riverine woods of bamboo, ivy, oleander, Judas, carob, plane and fig trees keep it wonderfully cool,

reach the 30-metre high WATER-FALL (**15min**), which looks very exotic — though bear in mind that the water has come from Shinolaka village and is not that clean! Return the same way (**30min**).

Walk b starts near the LIMESTONE QUARRY. *Do remember that this route was last checked in 2005!* With the quarry on your right, walk across the bridge and follow the track into the olive grove on the far side of the river. A couple of minutes past a *CAVE* and *DERELICT BUILDING* on the left, make your way to the *STREAM* (**5min**). From here, just follow the watercourse upstream as best you can! If it is flowing, it is essential that you have a stick, as the murky water prevents you seeing where you are placing your feet. Remember that there may be unseen rocks just below the surface, and that stones outside the main flow of the stream are more slippery than those in the middle. The deepest pools come after a few minutes, and again shortly before the aqueduct.

The watercourse bears right (southeast) and enters a small *GORGE*. After about 800 metres, you see a *CAVE* up to your right, with rickety ropes and ladders leading up to it (they looked unsafe in 2002). After another 400 metres, a left bend brings you face to face with the OTTOMAN AQUE-DUCT (**30min-1h**, depending on whether the stream is flowing or not). Return the same way (**1-2h**).

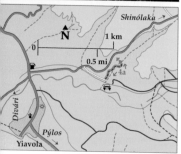

but also harbour mosquitoes. Cross the stream — in spring you will need to jump from rock to rock — and keep left, steeply up the far bank. Some steps carved in the earth, courtesy of Natura 2000 and an eco-minded schoolteacher from Pylos, may help. You quickly

46

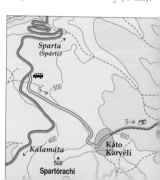

Walk 5: KATO KARVELI • KARVELI • LADA • ARTEMISIA

Distance/time: 11.6km/7.2mi; 5h15min

Grade: moderate, with ascents totalling 760m/2495ft and descents totalling 560m/1835ft, over stone paths and dirt tracks, steep in places. There is one passage which demands that you are sure-footed and have a head for heights.

Equipment: water, sunhat and sunscreen, picnic. A walking stick is useful for the rocky terrain, and long sleeves/trousers for the overgrown stretches.

Transport: 🚌 or 🚐 to Artemisia

(Car tour 2 at 61km/Timetables 6, 7). Then catch the morning bus from there towards Kalamata (Timetable 7), alighting at the turning to Kato Karveli. It is poorly signed and not a normal stop, so have your map handy and, if necessary, show the driver this: στην διακλαδωση για Κατω Καρβελι (Χανακια), 8 ΧΛΜ πανω απο την Καλαματα

Shorter walk: Kato Karveli — Karveli. 5km/3mi; 2h15min; easy. Just walk to Karveli; return to Kalamata or Kato Karveli by bus (Timetable 9) or taxi.

Despite its proximity to the popular Langada Pass road linking Kalamata and Sparta, the area of Alagonia is barely mentioned in guidebooks. Set amid splendid mountain scenery, the huddled villages and lush valleys have a genuinely isolated feel, matched by the inquisitive welcome of their inhabitants. Livestock and forestry are their mainstay — though sadly vast swathes of pines and firs are regularly burnt in accidental or politically-sparked forest fires — and the old paths we follow have (touch wood) largely escaped the ravages of the bulldozer.

Start the walk on the main KALAMATA–SPARTA ROAD, 8km above Kalamata: take the dirt track climbing gently east to 'KATO KARVELI 1.5KM'. In the desolate-looking hamlet of **Kato Karveli (20min)**, which is also called Hanakia (Little Inns), turn sharp left up a concrete lane, passing a carob tree on your right. At the end of the lane, keep straight on up a stony path which bends right to pass above the highest house in the village. This broad, part-paved mulepath winds steadily uphill through sparse kermes oak and

arbutus bushes, with the common *hosus negrus aquaforus* (black water hose) running intermittently

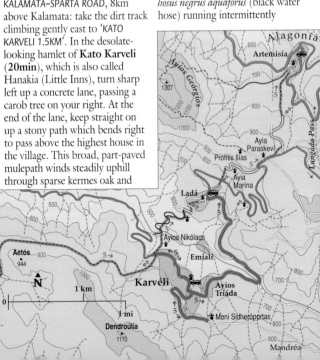

alongside. The views back over Kalamata and its bay spur you on through this relatively uninteresting part of the route. Blue waymarks guide you through a messy, stony section among old, WALLED FIELDS (**1h**). In autumn the red leaves and hairy fruit of the wig tree (*Cotinus coggygria*) stand out, while at ground level you may spot the red-and-cream globules of *Cytinus hypocistus*, a parasite which (as its name suggests) feeds off the roots of the cistus bush.

The path bears right and descends marginally into a valley before traversing visibly up the facing slope. Eventually (**1h30min**) you cross a pronounced spur and keep right, along the steep northern flanks of the peak named **Aetos** (Eagle), for reasons which can be occasionally seen gliding overhead. Ahead of you rises the summit of Ayios Georgios, with the village of Lada spilling triangularly down its right-hand flank. Further right you may just spot the high peak of Goupata (Neraïdovouna) poking up behind the main, wooded Taygetus ridge.

The clear, gravelly path crosses TWO ROCKY SPURS AND THREE BOULDER SPILLS (where you'll need a head for heights); it should always be passable, but take it carefully. Goats perch teasingly on the rocky outcrops above and below. After a THIRD ROCKY SPUR (**2h05min**), the path descends quite steeply towards Karveli (which is partly visible). At a HEAP OF BOULDERS (**2h15min**), ignore the path forking right and follow the original path down past a line of olive saplings. Squeeze past some prickly gorse and burnet bushes, with rockrose and lentisc adding their fragrances to the herbal mêlée. Just before meeting the road, the path veers right, keeping a stone's throw above it. At the first house of **Karveli**

(**2h45min**), keep straight on, passing under fig and loquat trees, to the ROAD (**2h48min**).

Here you could take a detour to the right, to the village centre and seasonal café (add 1km/15min return). Or continue past the café and then turn right where signed, to the charming, crumbling, cypress-ringed monastery of Sidheroportas (add 3.4km/40min return). If you prefer an easy road-walk to a tricky path, you can follow the main road all the way round the head of the valley to Lada (4km), where you would rejoin the route at the 3h47min-point.

The main walk turns left here and, after 100m, heads sharp right down a concrete path between telephone poles. Pass to the right of a house (**2h51min**), turn left behind it, and under a walnut tree bear right. You join a disused jeep track (**2h54min**) and keep right until, with the huge plane tree and chapel of **Ayios Nikolaos** visible 100m ahead, you fork left (**2h57min**) down a small, overgrown path waymarked with blue spots. This leads to another track, which you follow to the left for 50m, before forking right down the faint, squelchy continuation of the path (blue spots soon reappear). Keep right down the smaller path (**3h01min**; blue spot), which emerges next to an ARCHED BRIDGE across the stream (**3h07min**). Tall plane trees and dense ivy make this another cool rest spot.

Cross the bridge and continue straight on up the path, which cuts a corner off the track. Turn right onto a track into cypress woods (**3h13min**), where the old path cuts another corner. Follow the track right, past a CHURCH, and up to a junction with a concrete track (**3h23min**). Here, turn sharp right and after 30m sharp left up a stony, wet path. At the concrete

Above: on the path to Karveli; right: wig tree (Cotinus coggygria)

track (**3h33min**) turn left to a SPRING whose water (unlike any surface water) is drinkable and delicious. After this you turn sharp right up a stony path (blue spot). By the first house of **Lada** (**3h38min**), bear right, pass a church, and then go left up a concrete lane (**3h43min**). This joins the main road next to the large grey SCHOOL building and benches (**3h47min**). Cross the road and continue past the school and the CHURCH. After a short descent, turn left up a concrete lane (café) and follow the steepening lane up to the road (**4h03min**) by a SPRING and SHELTER. Cross over and — need I say it? — take the steeply climbing path into an olive grove, keeping right. At the track (**4h11min**), turn right and ignore the right fork to a shady chapel — or don't, if you feel like a rest. The concrete track eases off and joins the ASPHALT ROAD (**4h27min**). Follow this left to the 930m saddle and chapel of **Ayia Paraskevi** (**4h30min**) where, looking over the arrayed villages and hills of Alagonia, you can take a well-earned break.

From behind the church, a path descends to join a newly-bulldozed track, which leads left (north) towards Artemisia. The old, over-grown path affords short cuts in places. By a small METAL HUT on the left (**4h50min**), turn sharp right and, at the OLIVE GROVE (**4h52min**), sharp left through the woods. The track narrows to a path, descending to the uppermost houses of **Artemisia** (**5h02min**). Here turn left and immediately right, down a concrete lane through the village, keeping left at the small CHURCH. At the small SQUARE, bear right to emerge on the main road by LOULA MASOURIDI'S CAFE (ex-hotel), where the buses from Kalamata and Sparta meet and swop passengers (**5h15min**).

Walk 6: PROFITIS ILIAS • PIGADIOTIKO BRIDGE • PIGADIA • (KOSKARAKAS GORGE) • PROFITIS ILIAS

Distance/time: 12km/7.4mi; 4h30min. If returning along the gorge bed, add 1h.
Grade: moderate; a fairly flat walk, apart from the leg to Pigadia village (a climb/descent of 300m/1000ft). If returning along the gorge bed: strenuous, with difficult, boulder-filled terrain and an additional 200m/650ft climb at the end.
Equipment: sunscreen and hat, picnic, water, pullover. If returning along the gorge bed: sandals

and small foot towel for wading (springtime only), walking stick
Transport: 🚌 to/from Profitis Ilias (detour to Gaïtses on Car tour 2 at 16.8km). Park on the *rutted* dirt road below the chapel, near the shrine and sign 'Rintomo Canyon, only footpath'.
Shorter walk: Profitis Ilias — Pigadiotiko Bridge — Profitis Ilias. 9km/5.6mi; 3h; easy. Omit the 300m ascent to Pigadia, and return along the trail and dirt road.

T his walk takes you to one of the most breathtaking spots in the Taygetus range: the Pigadiotiko *yefiri* (bridge). This centuries-old stone span links the sheer walls of the Koskarakas (or Rindomo) Gorge at their narrowest point — about 10 metres apart, and twice that distance above the dark riverbed — in a wonderful combination of natural spectacle and human prowess. The hike starts below the panoramic church of Profitis Ilias near Vorio (one of the constituent hamlets of Gaïtses), and follows a dirt road and then an old mulepath to the bridge. There you can make a detour to the tiny hamlet of Pigadia, inhabited by a single 'guardian' shepherd, before returning to Profitis Ilias either along the dramatic, boulder-filled gorge bed (one stretch of wading) or, more easily, the way you came.

Start the hike below **Profitis Ilias**: notice the walking sign indicating the return route from the riverbed. Follow the dirt road uphill to a modern CHAPEL (**3min**), where you meet a larger dirt road. Turn left and after 700 metres fork left (**13min**). Follow this dirt road as it contours round two of the side-valleys feeding the main gorge; sporadic RED WAY-MARKS line the route. After another 1.5km turn left again at the sign 'KLHMA RINTOMO' (**40min**). About 700m further on the dirt road, hitherto just passable in a car, becomes too rough for any vehicle. Soon (**1h**) the track gives up completely and you continue on the delightful,

cobbled footpath, zigzagging down towards the gorge floor. You reach a CONCRETE BRIDGE across the narrow ravine (**1h10min**) — don't worry, this is not the bridge you have walked all this way to see! Continue two minutes down the path on your right to reach the old **Pigadiotiko Bridge** — two superimposed arches of unmortared stone, quite a feat of engineering, and still perfectly safe to cross (barring future earthquakes!). A further three minutes down a ramp of loose stones brings you to the floor of the **Koskarakas Gorge** (**1h15min**), with superb views back up between almost-touching cliffsides.

Profitis Ilias, where the walk begins. Sadly, the gate to the chapel yard is usually locked, but if it is open or you have managed to get the key from the papas in Vorio, the path up to it starts from a telephone pole southwest of the chapel. It's a worthwhile round trip of 15 minutes, with stunning views over this middle stretch of the Koskarakas (or Rindomo) Gorge. From the foot of the hill you can make out, among the terrace walls, a few massive blocks of dressed stone which may have come from a temple to Apollo.

Upstream from here — three full hours' hike away — lies the church of Panayia (Virgin Mary), dubbed 'Kapsadematousa' (Bale-Burner) when Our Lady, angered by the shepherds' uninterrupted hay-making on her feast day, made sparks fly out of the oxen's hooves and set fire to the dry bales. An hour beyond that lies the summer hamlet of Rindomo (whose name is sometimes used for the upper gorge), where a few shepherd families tend thousands of goats beneath the barren limestone flanks of Taygetus' high summits. You may meet them and their feta-laden mules on their way back to Gaïtses. Downstream lies the 'adventurous' return route along the gorge bed, which means a possible shower from a small waterfall, a short wade through knee-high water in spring, followed by two hours' athletic clambering down a boulder-filled gorge bed and 30-minute climb back out! But before you wonder whether to take the plunge or to return the way you came, it is worth following the mulepath up to the hamlet of Pigadia.

Cross the gorge on the concrete bridge (**1h20min**) and follow the path up the left (true right) bank of the side stream that descends from Pigadia. Goats passing overhead have kicked stones onto the path, so take it carefully. The zigzagging path crosses a small

CONCRETE BRIDGE (**1h35min**) to the opposite bank of the side-stream, and continues to climb steadily. It flattens out (**1h45min**) and you pass a seasonal POOL in the stream just deep enough for a glacial dip. On the opposite slope you can make out the tiny chapel of Ayia Paraskevi. The valley ahead is full of terraces where once the 200-strong population of Pigadia grew wheat, as the circular THRESHING FLOOR on the right (**1h55min**) suggests. From here a new dirt track runs above the old path, but the latter offers a more atmospheric arrival. Passing huge boulders, it bears right (where a small path descends left to some lovely springs) between proud, derelict houses, built of white limestone with grey slate rooves. The village 'square' at **Pigadia** (**2h05min**) makes a lovely picnic spot, with a tap, plane tree and the welcome coolness of 930m altitude. You may even come across the hardy shepherd who summers here with his 200 goats, making *sfela* cheese (a local variety of feta). Before you leave, climb up to the solidly-built stone church of **Taxiarches** (the Arch-angels; **2h10min**), perched on a rock overlooking the valley. Return the same way to the **Piga-**

Bouldery Koskarakas Gorge, with the two superimposed arches of Pigadiotiko Bridge crossing at the narrowest point. Do read all the notes below about the gorge bed return before you start out, then put the book away!

diotiko Bridge (**3h**) and retrace your route back to **Profitis Ilias** (**4h30min**).

Or, to return along the BED OF THE **Koskarakas Gorge**, turn left and left again to pass beneath the bridges: a chillingly dark and narrow natural corridor with slippery walls and floor. From about December to May you will need to wade through about 20 metres of glacial, calf-high water. There are two more narrow sections after this, with a chance of surface water in high spring, after which it is definitely safe to put your boots back on (**3h10min**). The gorge opens out. Pick your way as best you can over the rocks, looking out for CAIRNS. Further down, you'll find small IRON RUNGS to help you negotiate some small drops. At the first OVERHANGING BOULDER (**3h30min**), head left (rungs), cross to the far right (more rungs) or squeeze beneath a huge boulder; and again keep left (more rungs next to the vertical bank). The best route continues largely on the left, away from the bed. When you rejoin the bed (**3h50min**), look up to see the round dome of Profitis Ilias atop its cliff. When you come to a slippery rock in mid-bed (**4h05min**), keep briefly left, under the plane trees, before bearing right (two rungs). Soon (**4h15min**), with boulders projecting ahead, keep left down a four-runged slab. A small pool or mud-patch below parallel slanting strata heralds easier going (**4h35min**). Later (**4h50min**), where a big drop onto a pebbly strip forces you left, and with a water pipe just visible ahead, turn sharp left into the patch of plane trees bearing RED WAYMARKS (**4h55min**). A green sign announces that you are at **Avouros** (ΑΒΟΥΡΟΣ), almost directly below Profitis Ilias. On your right are stone benches, a picnic table and a tap. *Do not overshoot this spot or you will have to continue a further two hours before you can climb out of the gorge — at the stone bridge between Sotirianika and Kambos (Walk 7).*
From Avouros follow the jeep track climbing initially southeast, then back southwest. You can see the traces of old *kalderimi* (mule-path) beneath the surface. After 30 minutes' steady climb you will emerge by the SHRINE and sign 'RINTOMO CANYON, ONLY FOOTPATH' (**5h30min**).

55

Walk 7: SOTIRIANIKA • KAMBOS • (ZARNATAS CASTLE) • KARDAMYLI

See also photograph page 1
Distance/time: 15km/9.3mi;
4h50min (plus 3.5km/1h30min of
optional detours)
Grade: moderate. Good paths and
tracks over low hills, with about
300m/980ft climb and 600m/
1960ft descent
Equipment: water, sunhat,
sunscreen, picnic, swimming
things including sandals,
respectable clothes if visiting
Evangelistria nunnery, torch for
illuminating frescoes

Transport: 🚌 to Sotirianika (see
Car tour 2 at 22.2km). Park just
before the first large building on
the right. Or 🚐 to the Sotirianika
turn-off, 1km outside the village
(Kalamata–Kardamyli–Areopolis
route; Timetable 8). Return by the
same 🚐 from Kardamyli.
Shorter walk: Kambos to Kardamyli. 10km/6.2mi; 3h (plus
3.3km/1h15min of optional
detours); grade/access as main
walk. Follow the main walk from
the 1h55min point.

This is an excellent introduction to the Mani, combining
churches, castles, historic mulepaths, coastal scenery and
the chance of a swim. If you only have time for one walk in
the area, choose this one.

Start the walk at **Sotirianika**, at
the first large building* (after the
old school) on the right as you
approach the village. From the
double telephone pole next to the
building, follow the stone-laid
path up into the village, with a
fence on your left. In the village,
ignore alleys left and right; keep
straight on down a concrete path
and then up again into the second
part of the village. Continue out of

Sotirianika on a path descending
to a small CONCRETE BRIDGE and a
concrete road (**10min**). Turn right
along this, keeping right at the
first fork (**13min**) and left at the
second (**22min**).
Ignore a minor track off left but at
the next fork, 200m further on
(**30min**), keep left to reach the
ruined houses and SPRING of
Mavrinitsa (**32min**). The
concrete ends at this point. The

---

*The building is a modern OLIVE
PRESS, which operates every winter
and spring, producing oil for export
and crushed kernels for fodder and
low-grade frying oil. If it is open,
you can see into the left-hand room,
where 50kg sacks of small hard
olives (ελιες) and leaves from the
tree are emptied. Each sack produces
9-12kg of oil (λαδι), depending on
the fleshiness of the fruit. The first
machine strips the leaves (used as
fodder) off the branches, the second
separates and crushes the kernels
(κουκουτσια) which are sold for
about five cents per kg to be made
into kernel oil or fodder — you can
see this piling up outside the wall. A
third machine pulps, using two old
quernstones now powered auto-

matically, while the following
machines extract water and sludge.
The resulting oil is stored in five 30-
ton vats by the right-hand door,
awaiting export to Kalamata, Athens
or Austria. They don't export to
Italy, but accuse Italians of buying
pure Mani oil to add to their own,
thereby reducing the acidity until it
just qualifies for Virgin or Extra
Virgin status. Olives are harvested
from November to March, with
every second year providing a good
harvest. They are collected — mostly
by Albanian labourers — by raking
the fruit onto nets spread onto the
ground, or in some cases by feeding
cut branches into small machines
which separate fruit from foliage.

Above: the magnificent cobbled mule-path down into the Koskarakas Gorge; right: this lady in the ruined hamlet of Mavrinitsa is making sféla, *a locally-produced version of feta cheese.*

church of **Ayios Nikolaos**, which lies two minutes up to your left, is usually open and contains faded frescoes from the late 18th century. You can make out St Thanassis riding astride a large, human-faced fish surrounded by crabs, octopus and ships, as well as various beasts carrying human limbs in their mouths to Hades. The church belonged to an earlier monastery marked on some maps as St Panteleimon. The settlement was largely abandoned after the 1955 earthquake; a more violent one in 1986, which also left 10,000 Kalamatans homeless, finished it off.

Continue from the spring in the original direction. The path soon bends right and regains its former cobbles, zigzagging grandly down towards the valley floor. This *kalderimi*, or mulepath, is part of a network of two-metre wide stone roads built under the Ottomans in the 17th-18th centuries.

Sadly it peters out among lentisc bushes after a while, and you need to hop over to the right and walk parallel to it, dropping over disused terraces, before rejoining it

later. Soon you reach an impressive stone bridge across the **Koskarakas** (or Rindomo) **Gorge** (**55min**). Upstream soar red and grey cliffs dotted with swaying pines and guarded by falcons and kestrels. Further up lies the Piga-diotiko Bridge, shown on page 52 (Walk 6) and the tiny hamlet of Rindomo. Like other gorges of the Taygetus range, it is dry for about 300 days of the year, but there was once enough water to power a mill, whose ruins you can see on the far bank, down to the left.

Continue up the path climbing the far bank, ignoring a dirt track coming in from the west. At this point, the building on your left is a dilapidated OLIVE PRESS with the

Moní Ayios Georgiou

Altomirá

1000

900

7

400

500

600

700

800

máta

Sotiriánika

Prégana

Ayios
Nikólaos

Korakóspilo

Mavrinítsa

Koskárakas

600

Pigadiótiko
Bridge

200

Koskárakas

☀

📖
52

Koskárakas

600

358
▲

Profítis
Ilías

7

680
▲

Kapnisméno

759
▲

Evangelístria

Orovás

Gianísta

Vório (Gaïtsés)

📖
52

Poliánes

Ayii Theódorii

Kámbos

tavropígi

Zoodóchou
Pigís

300

Ayios Geórgios

Zárnatas
Castle

Ayios
Joannákis

ndourákis
Tower

Málta

Moní Androumbevítsis

Selimángouro

7

400

Ayios Konstandínos

694
▲

500

600

390
▲

300

200

Velónas

100

Glísas

7 7

Thomeíko

Lázos

Sóros
Panayía

Velónas
Bay

Kripiá

100

Kámbos

📖
60 8

N
▲

1 km

0

1 mi

Vírós

7

6

Kardamýli

9

Aerópolis

Ayios Dimítrios

Merópi

grindstone still *in situ*. The path follows a dip, still slippery in the morning shadow. When you join a dirt road at a right-angle, concrete-covered bend (**1h05min**), turn right. This descends to cross a small gully, passes an isolated farm, crosses a second stream (ignore two left turns) and climbs steeply to emerge on an unexpectedly broad ASPHALT ROAD (**1h35min**). To your right is the inconspicuous nunnery of **Evangelistria** (the Annunciation), inhabited by a single, elderly nun — though if you question her, she will reply, for fear of being robbed, that she has dozens of companions working in the fields nearby. If she is in and does not take you for a bandit, you may pop into the chapel, built as so often in front of a cave, light a candle and kiss (or admire) the miraculous, silver-plated icon of the Annunciation. You may also spot the earliest-known palindrome above the chapel entrance, ΝΙΨΟΝ ΑΝΟΜΗΜΑΤΑ ΜΗ ΜΟΝΑΝ ΟΨΙΝ ('wash not only my face but also my sins'), commonly found next to holy water. Follow the road, which climbs steadily; you can take a short cut on the left after 150m to avoid a small bend. The imposing church of Kambos comes into view across the olive groves. At the first houses

of **Kambos** (**1h50min**), keep left along a small lane parallel to the main road. After crossing the Gaïtses road, you reach the village square (**1h55min**), with its pair of cafes next to a 90° bend in the main road.

Detour 1 (20 minutes round trip): If you would like to see the smallest chapel in Messinia, go straight across the square and down ΑΓΙΟΥ ΚΟΝΣΤΑΝΤΙΝΟΥ, ignoring side alleys. After 250m (5min), turn right (signed CHURCH OF AYIOS IOANNIS). *The lane becomes a path. After 200m go through an unlocked gate on your right (10min) to see the miniature 13th-century chapel, usually known as* **Ayios Ioannakis** *(small St John), perched on top of a boulder. Return to Kambos square by the same route.*

To continue from the square, follow the main road west for 50m, towards the hill with the ruined castle of Zarnatas. On your right is the Byzantine chapel of **Ayii Theodorii** whose doors are usually open; if not, you'll have to enquire at one of the cafes on the square or at the house opposite for the key. The 18th-century frescoes which cover its interior walls feature more wild animals amongst their vivid depictions of damnation, salvation and lives of saints. The signs of the Zodiac —

Kambos, from Zarnatas Castle

Zarnatas Castle

a common feature in the Mani — refer to Christ's dominion over the stars, as part of the 'Ainoi' (Praises) cycle of frescoes (Psalm 148:3-4 'Praise ye him, sun and moon: praise him, all ye stars of light'). By the intricately-carved wooden iconostasis, you'll also see the two Saints Theodore, one on a white horse, one on a brown, signifying the 4th-century Roman soldiers and martyrs, Theodore Tyro and Theodore Stratelates. Turn right, past the west door of the church, and after barely 100m turn left on a concrete track. Ignore the right turn, and at the house keep left along a walled path which crosses a sewage-filled stream. Just before steps up to the main road (**2h**), follow the small path to the right for 50m, to a RUINED MANSION — home of the 19th-century Greek Prime Minister Alexandros Koumoundouros — and, more interestingly, the collapsed MYCENEAN BEEHIVE TOMB to its right, which may well be the mythological burial place of Mahaon, son of Asclepius and surgeon general of the Trojan Army. The presence of this tomb is a strong argument for this plateau being the location of Gerenia, an ancient town where Agamemnon was worshipped.

Return and climb the steps up to the MAIN ROAD (**2h05min**). Cross straight over and go up a stony path to a track (**2h08min**). Turn left here, then fork right uphill on concrete. Where the track peters out at a right bend (**2h15min**), turn left up a small path winding up in a southwesterly direction, with occasional red spots to help you. You emerge on another dirt track (**2h20min**); go left, to a concrete lane (perhaps signed to 'ZOODOCHOS PIGIS'; **2h25min**).

Detour 2 (30 minutes round trip): For the worthwhile walk to Zarnatas

Castle, follow the steep concrete lane right, up to a new house. Continue up a small path, first past a prickly pear plantation and then up overgrown hillsides. The castle is reached in a further 10 minutes, and at the time of writing can be entered freely, though look out for low door-arches and holes in the floor! Zarnatas rests on ancient foundations, presumably those of Gerenia's acropolis, and was subsequently fortified by the Byzantines, Franks and Turks, who built the present keep in 1670, along with a new perimeter wall and nine bastions (now ruined). They only held it for 14 years before the Venetian count Morosini took it by siege, successfully intercepting Turkish messengers and supplies, in his short-lived bid to recapture the Peloponnese. By 1805, when British Captain Leake visited, it was in ruins, and shortly afterwards a new castle was built by the Maniots — that of Kapetanakos, visible on a hilltop to the north — to defend themselves from the Turks in Kalamata. The views from here take in much of the Taygetus range, dominated by the rugged 2203-metre peak of Halasmeno Vouno, with the villages of Kambos, Stavropigio and Malta spread below you. Just 100m northwest of the castle is the (usually locked) chapel of Zoodochou Pigis. Return the same way to the concrete lane.

To continue, turn left along the lane, which curves right. Follow this past the CHURCH at the top of **Malta** village (**2h30min**) — named, perhaps, when this area was mortgaged to the knights of

St John in the 19th century. The lane leaves the village.

***Detour 3** (15 minutes return): 300m after Malta church, a small path climbs up right, to the semi-ruined tower of **Koumoundourakis**, with jagged crenellations, gargoyles, machicolations (holes for pouring burning oil) and the private chapel shown on page 1. In later centuries it provided the best point from which to besiege Zarnatas with artillery.*

The lane brings you to the main road opposite a BUS SHELTER and SHRINE (**2h40min**). Turn right (yes, right) and after 70 metres turn left onto a concrete road. After 200 metres turn left, up a steep concrete track (BLUE AND YELLOW ARROW). At the PASS (**2h50min**) you can see the coast of the Messinian Mani stretching away before you. In the distance is the steep seaward slope of the mountain of Osios Nikon — the 9th-century saint who finally converted the Maniots to Christianity. In the middle distance is the town of Kardamyli, distinguished by the chimney of its disused olive soap factory. On the first ridge in line with Kardamyli is the roofless church of Panayia, which lies on our onward route.

Follow the winding track — first concrete, then dirt — downhill for 2.5km (a good half hour). In places the old mulepath cuts corners, indicated by BLUE AND YELLOW WAYMARKS. At the end of a long straight stretch, where the track bends slightly right (**3h25min**), look out for a BLUE AND YELLOW WAYMARK indicating your little ongoing path climbing the steep left bank.

***Detour 4** (35 minutes round trip): If you feel like a swim and have the time and energy, it is a further 1.2km (15 minutes) down the track to the small, pebbly cove of **Velonas**, where you are almost guaranteed to be alone. Bear in mind that there is no shade, and you will need sandals (or tough feet) to get into the water. And, of course, it is uphill on the way back!*

Follow the waymark up the left bank, past a line of olive trees, then bear right and intercept the old mulepath once more. A little overgrown in places, this climbs steadily towards the ridge, with lovely views over Velonas Bay. One zigzag and you reach the crest called '**Soros**' and the roofless, slit-windowed church of **Panayia** (**3h45min**).

After a rest, continue along the trail — less conspicuous now — to a gravel track (**3h50min**). Here you can choose between the rockier but more direct mulepath, which continues just to your left (BLUE AND YELLOW WAYMARK), or the smoother but more sinuous gravel track. If you take the path, you cross the road once (**3h55min**), two more times in close succession (**4h**), and a fourth time (**4h10min**). After this fourth crossing, keep your eyes open for an unexpectedly sharp right turn on a slab of rock, to rejoin the road by a newly-built stone house. However you reach this house (**4h20min**), it is worth squeezing through the bushes on your right just below it (BLUE AND YELLOW WAYMARK) to rejoin the path and follow it over a STONE BRIDGE across a surprisingly deep ravine, which hides nesting owls. You soon come alongside a concrete track (**4h25min**) and follow this down past a couple of houses into the olive groves at sea level. By the low stone walls, fork right to the shingly BEACH (**4h35min**). Follow the coast road south, crossing the dry bed of the river **Viros**, to join the main road through **Kardamyli** next to its white-washed CHURCH (**4h50min**). The main part of the village is a few minutes to your right.

Walk 8: KARDAMYLI • VIROS GORGE • LYKAKI MONASTERY • TSERIA • EXOHORI • AYIA SOFIA • KARDAMYLI

Distance/time: 14km/8.7mi; 6h20min

Grade: strenuous, with an ascent from sea level to 600m/1970ft and back again, and with a further 100m climb/descent thrown in for good measure. The terrain is rocky, especially in the Viros Gorge, and there is little shade. The path between Tseria and Exohori requires a head for heights. But the paths are mostly clear, and the cobbled trails a delight to tread on.

Equipment: strong boots, water, sunhat, sunscreen, picnic (or good enough Greek to order a snack meal in Tseria/Exohori). A walking stick is useful for the rocky terrain, and long trousers for the undergrowth.

Transport: 🚗 to/from Kardamyli (base for Car tour 2) or 🚌 to Kardamyli (Timetables 8, 10, 11)

Alternative walks: To avoid some or almost all of the ascent, start in **Kalives** (🚌 Timetable 10 or taxi) or **Tseria** (taxi) and walk the rest of the way via Exohori to Kardamyli (moderate; respectively 11km/6.8mi; 5h and 8km/5mi; 3h30min). Alternatively, if you want a longer stretch through the **Viros Gorge**, turn right at the 4h45min point and later pick up the outgoing route.

This walk describes a loop around the lower Viros Gorge, starting and ending in the coastal town of Kardamyli and passing two villages which face each other across the gorge. You start with a short section along the gorge bed, then climb over bushy hillsides to the scattered village of Tseria, drop steeply to cross the gorge where the high Taygetus mountains start, climb briefly to Exohori village, and finally descend through olive groves and open land to Ayia Sofia church and then Kardamyli. All in all, you should be in good shape, and start early, if you are to do the whole loop.

Start out by following the main road north through **Kardamyli** and, at the SUPERMARKETS, fork right down a small lane (green sign 'AGIA SOFIA' and brown sign 'KARDAMYLI OLD TOWN'). Ignore the right turn to Ayia Sofia and keep left up a gravel track (yellow

In the Viros Gorge near Sotiros Monastery (one of the Alternative walks)

Lykaki Monastery; its setting is safe, sylvan and serene.

sign 'TSERIA 32'), dropping down to the riverbed where possible. You can see the old town of Kardamyli on your right. Follow the riverbed, or a path next to it, inland (northeast). BLUE AND WHITE WAYMARKS indicate the best route along the **Viros Gorge**. After a cypress tree in the middle of the bed, you come across a small SPRING (dry in autumn) and shady walnut tree under an overhang (**35min**). Soon (**40min**) a waymark guides you up the left (true right) bank; you pass a cypress grove, cross the riverbed again and, at a BLUE AND WHITE ARROW, rise up the right (true left) bank. The small path winds up through scrubby woods of kermes oak, lentisc and maple for a few

minutes, before easing off, joining another path and returning to river level by a STONE WALL and a blue-white arrow (**55min**). Keep left here, climbing a small path towards the cypress trees visible ahead. They surround the semi-ruined monastery of **Lykaki** (Small Wolf; **1h**), whose cruciform *katholikon* (church) is intact but locked. The outbuildings and perimeter wall have largely crumbled. The monastery probably dates from the 16th century and has been unoccupied since the 19th. If you do locate the key to the church, you'll see faded, naïve 18th-century frescoes of torture scenes, the crucifixion and various saints, including St Demetrius appearing to ride his horse back to front.
Return the same way to the riverbed and continue inland. Occasional waymarks point to a faint path on the right (true left)

side of the riverbed. After 10 minutes (**1h15min**), beneath a rocky crag on the left, and with a faint jeep track coming down from Ayia Sofia on the right, turn left up a small path with RED AND WHITE WAYMARKS, passing under two carob trees. This bears left, crosses a gully and climbs stonily and increasingly steeply back to the west. A FENCE runs along on your left, and the path becomes a jeep track, with the village of Prosilio visible ahead. After 15 minutes' climb (**1h30min**) the path levels out among the olive groves below **Kalives** village; follow the green 'PEDINO' sign to the right, along a path between groves, with occasional red and white waymarks.

After a further 30 minutes' steady climb through lentisc and kermes bushes, the old cobbled path levels off and offers open views across the canyon to Exohori village and the cragtop chapel of Ayios Georgios (**2h**). When you join a dirt track at a CONCRETE-COVERED HAIRPIN BEND (**2h15min**), keep right, downhill. After a couple of minutes, take a left fork, which soon becomes a flattish path overgrown with cistus, bee orchids, Malcolm's cress, salsify, thistles and various vetches and peas, including the pink-flowering pitch trefoil (so called because when crushed it stinks of tar). Cross a STONE BRIDGE and climb a broad paved section of path. This takes you to the first house of **Pedino** (ΠΕΔΙΝΟ; **2h40min**), the lowest part of Tseria. Follow the concrete path east through the village to the CHURCH, and pass to the right of it, up a concrete lane. At the fork (**2h45min**) keep right to pass under a large oak tree. The main part of Tseria is visible up to your left, against the barren, stony flanks. You pass the hamlet of **Katafigio** (Refuge) on your right,

perched above the cave-riddled cliffs where locals once hid from Turks, barricading themselves in with stone walls for extra security. At the left-hand hairpin bend (**2h52min**), continue straight on up a path with tight zigzags. Rejoin the concrete lane and turn right, passing through **Zaharias** hamlet and climbing steadily. After the last house of Zaharias (**3h05min**), where the road bends left to **Yiatreika**, turn sharp right up a concrete track (green sign 'VYROS GORGE'; RED AND WHITE WAYMARK). The name Yiatreika means 'doctor', suffixed with a Slavic ending, and has been linked with the Medici of Florence. Where the track bends sharp left back to **Tseria** (**3h10min**)*, continue right/straight (green sign 'VYROS GORGE') along a level path. The path continues level for five minutes, with lovely views far ahead to the pyramidal peak of Aï Lias or Profitis Ilias, Taygetus' highest at 2400m (nearly 8000 feet). Then, with the gorge at your feet, it starts its sinuous 200-metre descent. The surface is part-paved and reasonably well used, but fairly steep and potentially vertiginous. After 25 minutes (**3h 40min**), fork right (RED AND BLUE WAYMARK) downhill, to reach the gorge bed by a wall. Just before the bed there are some big steps

---

*If you are starting the walk in Tseria, you will probably be dropped in the main part of the village, and should follow the lane south through the village towards Yiatreika, passing a large TOWERLESS CHURCH on the right. At the first houses of Yiatreika, fork left up a stepped path through the hamlet, passing to the right of a SMALL CHURCH on the square of ΙΑΤΡ. ΜΕΔΙΚΩΝ. Where the lane bends sharp right, keep left/straight along the level path (green sign, red and white waymark) and continue as the main walk.

down a steep boulder spill. Pick your way down the bed for 100m, to the end of the wall on your left (**3h50min**); then scramble up past the bottom of the wall and steeply up the left bank (red and blue waymarks). The path bends left, crosses some boulders and reaches a WATER SERVICE TRACK.

Strange as this may seem in such a parched riverbed, the area just downstream was once full of water mills which ground the corn grown on the plateaux above. The trickles of water — it only ever flows heavily after a big storm combined with spring snowmelt — were gathered in a mud-lined conduit and passed from mill to mill. Now a big black hose takes water from springs further upstream and pipes it straight to the tourist centres on the coast for us to have twice-daily showers, leaving the intermittent land far drier than nature intended.

Follow the water service track uphill, keeping left at the fork, and climbing steadily towards Exohori, with views across to the cliffs below Yiatreika. You you pass a SHRINE up to the left (**4h15min**), signalling that the worst of the 100m climb is over. The track dips slightly, then climbs past a large rusting sign alerting you to the PANORAMA (in case you have not seen it). At at fork (**4h27min**), go right, down through **Kolibet-seika**, the first of the hamlets that make up Exohori. Where the now-surfaced lane bends left, fork right past the hotel and reroofed CHURCH. Continue down a walled lane, past a broad concrete parking area, and into the hamlet of **Hora**, passing to the right of its CHURCH. A concrete lane joins from the left (**4h40min**). If you want to explore the central part of **Exohori**, follow this left, past the school and across the asphalt road, returning the same way. Other-

wise keep straight on, down ΟΔΟΣ ΒΑΣ ΤΡΙΒΟΥΡΕΑ.

The name Exohori, pronounced 'Xohóri' by locals, means 'outer village'; but in the middle ages, when its population numbered around 5000, it went by the name Androuvista (or Ardouvitsa, or any variant thereof). Its inhabitants were the Slavic Melingi, who also dominated the valleys behind Mystras on Mt Taygetus' eastern slopes, but who by 1400 had embraced Greek language and Orthodoxy. Situated at the foot of the forested slopes of Mt Marathos, it earned a reputation for carpentry, particularly wooden washboards. Its family chapels (which locals claim number one hundred) and its well-built houses (likewise one thousand) display folkloric carvings of animals and trees.

The lane soon becomes a paved path in a dip. Up to your left is the chapel of **Ayios Nikos** (probably Osios Nikon), where, after a late introduction to Orthodoxy and the mystic beauty of rural Greece, the travel writer Bruce Chatwin chose to be buried. With a mulberry tree and clearing ahead, fork left (RED AND WHITE ARROW; **4h45min**). (*Turning right here would lead via the cragtop chapel of Ayios Georgios down to Sotiros Monastery in the Viros Gorge, with blue and white waymarks to guide you — one of the Alternative walks, illustrated on page 59.*)

When you join an earthy track (**4h50min**), keep straight on/right, leaving the shady olive groves behind you. Where the track bends right (**4h55min**), fork left by a stone wall, soon passing two WHITE-CROSS-ON-RED WAYMARKS (like the Swiss flag). You may spot ruts from old carts carrying locally quarried *porólithos* stone. Pass to the right of the small chapel of **Ayia Paraskevi**

The pyramidal peak of Profitis Ilias, from the path east of Yiatreika

(5h05min) and cross straight over the same track twice. Follow the waymarks carefully down rocky slabs among scrub and sparse olive saplings. When you rejoin the track (5h15min), keep left/straight on, passing the new, tiled chapel of **Ayii Pantes** (All Saints). After this, fork right down a smaller track (HIDDEN WAYMARK), which turns into a path. Suddenly (5h25min) a dirt road appears directly below your feet: turn sharp left and follow the carefully placed stone steps down to it, turning left when you get there. At the asphalt road (waymarks and small signpost to MONH ΣΩΤΗΡΑ), turn right to the visible houses of **Ayia Sofia** (locally called Gournitsa). Follow the concrete track through the village to the elegant, tall-domed chapel of **Ayia Sofia** or Holy Wisdom (5h40min). It is locked, but the key holder Eleni lives in the village and, if you speak some Greek, may agree to show you the carved iconostasis and early 18th-century frescoes.

By the WHITE METAL SIGNPOST near this chapel, turn sharp right (YELLOW AND BLACK ARROW) down a paved path. At the track (5h45min), with a twin vaulted niche cut in to the rock on your right, turn sharp left and immediately fork right down a paved path (HIDDEN WAYMARK). You pass the squared-off base of a MEDIEVAL TOWER on the left, under the cliffs of the Mycenean and medieval acropolis of Kardamyli. Just after a left bend (6h), give your pounding feet a rest and examine the twin vaulted niches cut into the rock on your left, gated with a black grille. Could these be, as many claim, MYCENEAN TOMBS and the supposed resting places of Castor and Pollux, the heavenly twins whom we know as Gemini and the Greeks as Dioscouri?

Continue down to the OLD, WALLED PART OF **Kardamyli** (6h10min), which is worth a visit if you have not already seen it. Go through the arch, into the square where anti-Turk insurgent Kolokotronis reputedly played chess, using real soldiers as pieces, with local chieftain Mourtzinos; passing the lovely 18th-century CHURCH of Ayios Spiridon on the right and the TOWER HOUSES of the Mourtzinos-Troupakis clan (supposedly descended from the Byzantine Paleologos dynasty) on the left. Follow the path bearing left, past the small summer café, and turn right by two cypresses (BLACK AND YELLOW WAYMARK). Cross the track and the stone bridge, and follow the recently paved path to the FIRST HOUSES OF **Kardamyli** (6h20min). Keep straight (left) to join the main road near the white CHURCH.

Walk 9: KARDAMYLI • PETROVOUNI • PROASTIO • KALAMITSI BEACH • KARDAMYLI

Distance/time: 7.5km/4.7mi; 2h45min
Grade: easy, though the 200m/ 650ft descent to Kalamitsi is rocky and is awkward when overgrown
Equipment: water, sunhat, snacks, swimming things including sandals
Transport: 🚗 (base for Car tour 2) or 🚌 to/from Kardamyli (Timetables 8, 10, 11)

This is a lovely short circular walk from the coastal town of Kardamyli. The route heads up through olive groves to two inland villages and then back down to the sea at Kalamitsi Beach, offering a chance for a refreshing swim before returning to Kardamyli.

Start the walk at the main CHURCH of **Kardamyli**: follow the main road south through the village towards STOUPA. After 500m (**8min**), by the municipal buildings, turn left up an asphalt lane (green sign 'PETROVOUNI, ST SOPHIA'). The lane passes the Hotel Esperides on the left. Some 150 metres after a right bend (**20min**), turn sharp left up a path (GREEN SIGN AND RED-WHITE ARROW) which joins the old, zigzagging mulepath (having ignored the earlier concrete road that offers another route up to Petrovouni). The steady gradient and 2-metre wide cobbled surface make this *kalderimi* a delight to walk on, with lovely views over Kardamyli, her olive groves and the tall chimney of her old soap factory.

At the first house of **Petrovouni** (**35min**), turn right and pass in front of it, following a path with a low rockface on your left. A left bend takes you into the little SQUARE of this hamlet (**45min**), with its mulberry tree. Keep right and then turn left along the main road, passing the locked 18th-century church of **Faneromeni** (Apparition of the Virgin Mary) on your right. This is one of a chain of delightful, tall-domed chapels capping the escarpment above Kardamyli; two others are

visible to the north (Karaveli and Ayia Sofia). The pyramidal peak of Taygetus and the forested summit of Mavrovouni soar up ahead.

Shortly before a left bend, fork right (**50min**) up a concrete lane which becomes a dirt/gravel track. In spring it is lined with flowering cistus bushes and tall salsify stems. Cistus (rock rose) leaves exude a resin in the midday heat which medieval monks — perhaps from the small monasteries attached to Karaveli or Faneromeni — used to collect with leather rakes in order to make a myrrh-like perfume. Salsify, which is also called goat's beard (or *tragopogon* in Greek) because of its hairy bud, has sweet-tasting roots which were eaten, boiled, by the ancient Greeks — and still are in some parts of the country.

Ignore a track to the right (**57min**) and keep straight on, parallel to a fence on the left (NO WAYMARK). The fence soon bears off to the left, after which you fork right along a path under the olive trees (WAYMARK), passing a rutted rock-bed — perhaps from carting the stone which was quarried near here — and a MINIATURE CHAPEL built of dressed stone. One can easily imagine that the rectangular slabs come from an ancient temple base, for it is a magical spot.

Karaveli Church in Petrovouni, with Profitis Ilias peak in the background

Pass to the right of the chapel door on a path bearing right, through a gap in a low stone wall, and then bear left (sporadic waymarks). At the end of the olive grove, turn left down a jeep track between two small stepped BASINS (**1h10min**). These are old quarries where a porous stone called *porólithos* was extracted and dressed for cornerstones. Pass to the left of a RUINED BUILDING, then veer left along a flat path. Where this crosses a band of rock, bear right (faded waymark) towards the visible cypresses and church of Ayios Georgios Monastery near Proastio. The 'path', such as it is, drops over rocky ground, then flattens out past a clump of cypresses and some natural overhangs (**1h20min**). Amidst these, easily missed, is a CAVE-CHAPEL with a resident hoopoe and deteriorating frescoes of, among others, the Archangel Michael and the fervent 9th-century Maniot proselytizer (Osios) Nikon.

Shortly after this, you drop into the thickly vegetated gully of **Lozni** on your right and continue along its left bank. Here you will encounter sage, cistus, broomrape and orchids galore in spring. In an olive grove (**1h30min**), follow the path left, uphill, towards two adjacent cypress trees on the skyline (NO WAYMARK). In front of these, turn right; then, by a waymarked olive tree, left up to the walled church of **Ayios Georgios** (**1h40min**). This former monastic church, now inhabited by a little owl, contains 18th-century frescoes of St George, the crucifixion, the temptation of Adam and Eve, and the omnipresent Mary and Christchild. Follow the jeep track towards Proastio, past more *porólithos* quarries. You can short-cut right along a path which cuts steeply down some rocky steps and up again to the main road by the village limit road sign. This route is waymarked.

Either way, at the asphalt road, turn right, into **Proastio** (**1h50min**). Despite the fact that its name, locally pronounced 'Prastío', means 'suburb', this was once a sizeable town, larger than Kardamyli, and the seat of a bishop. It has over 30 family chapels, plus an unusually large parish church, and lots of sturdily built houses using the local porous

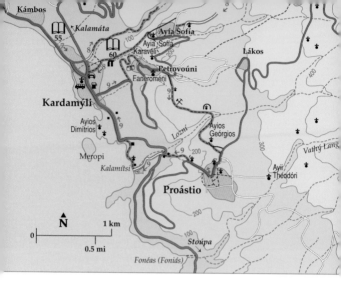

stone. Its situation — a short way inland, atop an escarpment yet camouflaged from the pirates who regularly raided the coast until the 19th century — may have contributed to that wealth. When some inhabitants moved to the isle of Meropi off Kardamyli, they were quickly besieged by Turks from Koroni.

In the village centre, by a bend in the road, you reach the church of **Ayios Nikolaos** on the right (**2h**). The church was restored both internally and externally between 2001 and 2005. As a result, paranoia of theft or vandalism means that the church is permanently locked. To attempt to get hold of the key (or to visit one of the two village *kafenia* still operational), head down the alley opposite the church to the main square. Here you need to locate the priest (*'O Papas'*) to get hold of the key.

The route continues from Agios Nikolaos along the main road heading out of the village, passing a mini-market and then a PLAYGROUND and SPRING on your right. At a small, white-washed CHAPEL (**2h06min**), follow the GREEN WALKERS SIGN TO KALAMITSI

to descend a steep rocky path that zigzags its way down to the main road.

The path emerges on the main road by two new stone houses (**2h25min**). Turn right and fairly immediately sharp left down a concrete road to the beach for a possible swim stop — **Kalamitsi Beach** is pebbly and good for snorkelling.

Just before reaching the beach, you may have noticed a dirt path heading off to the right. Return to this path and follow it northwards. It runs alongside the garden walls of Sir Patrick Leigh Fermor's house. The path snakes through the olive groves, past a small CHAPEL and the Hotel Kalimitsi to emerge on a sharp bend in the main road. Follow the road back to **Kardamyli** high street (**2h45min**).

Walk 10: PANAYIA YIATRISSA MONASTERY • MILIA • (ELEOHORI) • AYIOS NIKOLAOS

Distance/time: 12.5km/7.8mi; 5h
Grade: moderate; little ascent, but a descent of over 1000m/3300ft, mostly on stony paths
Equipment: sunhat and sunscreen, water, picnic, walking stick, swimming things
Transport: 🚗 with friends or a taxi to Panayia Yiatrissa (Car tour 2, Alternative return route at 163km); it's about 100km (2h 30min drive) from Ayios Nikolaos via Areopolis and Gython. 🚌 (for the dedicated only; Timetable 14) from Gython to Kastania and walk up the road (4km) to Yiatrissa. To return: 🚌 (early afternoon) from Ayios Nikolaos to Gython via Itilo and Areopolis (Timetables 8, 16, 18).
Alternative walks:
1 Milia — Ayios Nikolaos.
8km/5mi; 3h; easy. 🚌 (Timetable 13) or taxi from Kardamyli or

Stoupa to Milia. Pick up the main walk at the 1h35min-point and follow it to the end, taking a 🚌 (Timetable 10) or taxi back.
2 Milia — Yiatrissa — Milia — Ayios Nikolaos. 16km/10mi; 7h; fairly strenuous, with an ascent of 550m/1800ft and descent of 1100m/3600ft. Transport as for Alternative walk 1. Walk up to Yiatrissa, back again and down to Ayios Nikolaos. From the square in the main part of Milia village, start along the road heading towards Kariovouni and after three minutes fork right up a concrete lane (green sign 'Monastery of Virgin Mary the Healer' ie Yiatrissa). After another three minutes fork left down a path and follow the blue waymarks all the way to the monastery (2h). Pick up the main walk notes below and follow it to the end.

T his is a delightful way of crossing from Laconia (the eastern side of Taygetus) into Messinia (the western) via one of the lower passes in the range, around 1000m. Along the way you follow historic footpaths, pass the forgotten villages of Milia and Eleohori, and end up at a small, sandy beach. The snag? Finding somebody to drive you round the mountain, or paying for a taxi (see 'Transport'). A pre-emptive word about Yiatrissa: don't expect a picturesque Byzantine church tended by friendly monks; it's windswept, ugly and empty. Just enjoy the views!

The walk begins at the monastery of **Panayia Yiatrissa** (Virgin Mary the Healer). Looking like a space-ship that has just landed, the building is a huge, grey monstro-sity straddling the windswept, barren Taygetus ridge at one of its lowest points (1050m). Its windowless perimeter walls are firmly locked, except around the 15th August when the feast of Our Lady's Dormition is celebrated. But the views, westwards over the rugged valleys of Milia to the Messinian Sea, and eastwards over

Gython, the Laconian plain and its gulf, are suitably divine.
From the monastery follow the WATERSHED south for 300 metres (**5min**); then, just before the fir trees, turn right (BLUE ARROW AND 'M') down a stony path. The going improves as you enter the firs, and the blue waymarks I painted in 2002 should help your route-finding. After 15 minutes' steady descent, you pass a SPRING shaded by a fig tree on your left (**20min**). The water is deliciously cool. The path descends another 30 metres,

bears left and levels off briefly before descending again, now partly cobbled. Orchids, euphorbia and sage flowers liven up the path, while oak and broom bushes lend the opposite hillsides some colour. At the VALLEY FLOOR (**40min**) the path starts switching from side to side like a Maniot mercenary. It stays on the left bank initially, then crosses to the right bank (*BLUE WAYMARKS;* **44min**), back to the left (**53min**), to the right (**56min**), the left (**59min**), passes through a makeshift gate, and finally — for all Maniots are royalist at heart — plumps for the right (**1h03min**). Pass to the right of a BREEZE-BLOCK GOAT BARN (**1h07min**) and continue along a jeep track. Two minutes after this, at a right bend, turn sharp left (*easily missed*) down a bulldozed trail now covered in plants. Where this ends, cross the rubble and continue along a smaller, slightly overgrown path with a gully on your left side. At the junction with a larger path (**1h15min**), keep

left, past a small CHAPEL and across a lovely little STONE BRIDGE. At the concrete lane (**1h30min**), turn right, down to the asphalt road, which leads left into the square of central **Milia** (**1h35min**).

There is a simple café on your left, and next to it a beautiful Byzantine cruciform CHURCH with a Venetian belltower and symbolic bas-relief carvings. Both are open sporadically and can offer, respectively, cold drinks and snacks, or a cycle of 18th-century frescoes featuring (among others) a Turk sitting alongside a white-suited Venetian as Judges of the Earth.

Like many Maniot villages, Milia is composed of several *sinikíes* (hamlets), usually called by their most common family surnames. The central one, where you are now, is **Fakrianika**, where anti-Turk hero Kolokotronis spent a part of his childhood. The highest, Xanthianika, lies up to your left. The lowest, Kato Hora ('lower place') lies below to your right,

and is your next port of call. To reach it, continue along the concrete road heading west (towards KIVELIA) and after four minutes (**1h39min**) turn right down a well-paved path passing to the left of the disused four-windowed SCHOOL building. In front of the telephone pole (**1h43min**) the path, almost invisible in spring beneath carpets of cerinthe and malcolmia, bends right, then left, then right again. On your way down you pass to the right of a ruined house and adjacent Byzantine chapel dedicated to **Ayios Ioannis o Prodromos** (John the Baptist). Continuing down, you cross a STONE BRIDGE (**1h52min**) and bear left, following the concrete lane to the shady central square of **Kato Hora** (**2h**).

Just after the CHURCH, cross the square and turn left along a concrete path (GREEN SIGN AND BLUE WAYMARK). Follow the main path, flat at first, then climbing briefly past a small white-washed

chapel dedicated again to **Panayia Yiatrissa**. At a carob tree (**2h10min**), fork left, downhill (*no signpost*). The part-paved path soon resumes an intermittent climb, until at its highpoint (**2h35min**) you can see the hamlet of Eleohori atop a cliff in the middle distance. On the highest hump of the nearer ridge, you can distinguish the tiny chapel of Ayios Georgios — God only knows how it got there.

Follow the path zigzagging down, then straightening out with a small gorge on your left. You pass a ruined house on your right, and soon afterwards reach a shady, flat shoulder (**2h50min**). Here, go through the WOODEN GATE on your right and follow the stone-laid path as it winds down through intermittent oak woods and bursts of cyclamen. At the streambed, turn left and then right at the WALKERS' SIGN. At the jeep track turn left, uphill, and follow it left as it climbs through olive groves. At the first right-hand hairpin

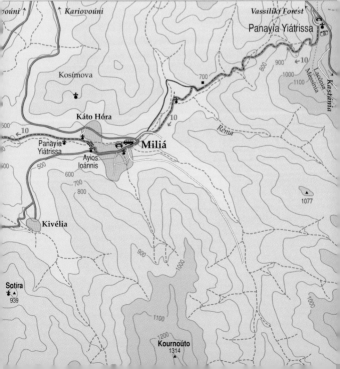

(3h15min), keep straight on along a paved path. There is another mini-gorge down to your left, which might trouble you if you suffer acutely from vertigo. Eventually (3h30min) you join a concrete road by a green sign pointing back to 'Milea'.

Detour: The tiny village of Eleohori (Izna) lies a few minutes up to your right. If you decide to explore it, you will pass a café (open sporadically) on the left, before climbing the hill in a clockwise curl to reach the clifftop church which you saw earlier. The views are dramatic; the church (usually locked) less so.

The main walk follows the concrete road downhill (left) to Riglia. At the first houses of **Ano Riglia** (3h55min), fork right on a concrete path (by a derelict house on the right). At the 'square', greet any bemused, wizened faces with a smile and keep straight on down the path, passing the village CHURCH (and heavily laden orange trees) on your left. When you rejoin the road (just over **4h**), continue downhill. After 200 metres (4h05min) turn sharp right down a concrete road, across a bridge and into **(Kato) Riglia**. At the square and CARDPHONE (4h10min), turn left past the café. At the main road (you could possibly pick up a bus here), turn left, and after 100 metres go right, down an asphalt lane marked ΠΑΡΑΛΙΑ ΠΑΝΤΑΖΙ. You pass several unfinished houses and meet the COAST ROAD BETWEEN AYIOS NIKOLAOS AND TRAHILA (4h25min). In front of you is a sandy beach with tamarisk trees and a summer café which serves excellent cool drinks. After a well-earned swim, turn right along the coast road into the centre of **Ayios Nikolaos** (4h50min), locally still called by its Slavic name, Selinitsa. It has a pretty fishing harbour with cafes, shops and a single taxi. The BUS STOP is at the far (north) side of the harbour (5h).

The flower- and Euphorbia-lined path between Milia and Kato Hora

Walk 11: ITILO • DEKOULOU MONASTERY • NEO ITILO BEACH • AREOPOLIS • PIRGOS DIROU SEA-CAVES

Distance/time: 11.8km/7.3mi; 4h
Grade: moderate, with a steep descent from 200m/650ft (Itilo) to sea level (Neo Itilo), a steady climb back to 200m/650ft (Areopolis), and another descent to sea level (the caves). The terrain is a mixture of small paths, cobbled mulepath and tracks.
Equipment: water, sunhat and sunscreen, picnic. A walking stick is useful for the rocky terrain, and long sleeves/trousers for the overgrown stretches. A jumper for the caves (it is a cool 15°C within). Money for a donation to Dekoulou (or a small gift for the children).

Transport: See logistics/suggestions in the main text below.
🚗 Itilo is on Car tour 2, just north of Areopolis; the caves are on Car tour 3, just south of Areopolis. There are many taxis in Areopolis. To return: 🚌 from the caves to Areopolis (Timetable 15); also from Areopolis to Itilo (Timetable 16)
Shorter walk: Itilo to Areopolis. 7.8km/4.8mi; 2h45min; moderate). End the walk at Areopolis and catch the 🚌 back to Itilo.

T his walk has a bit of everything. It starts with a wonderfully frescoed monastic chapel, a sandy beach, a well-preserved stretch of old cobbled road and some fine coastal views. Areopolis, when you get there, is a busy village with a historic centre and churches galore. If this isn't enough, you can continue down to the breathtaking sea-caves near Pirgos Dirou. Being punted through over 1000 metres of dark, subterranean waterways by a modern Charon, spooky stalactites gliding by at every turn, is the stuff of Orphean dreams. But beware the crowds. On summer mornings, especially at weekends, there can be queues of over an hour to visit the caves. I suggest doing the walk in the morning and visiting the caves in the afternoon, after the crowds have gone (current opening times are: June-Sept: 08.00-17.15, Oct-May: 08.30-14.45; closed Mondays). Out of season, it is fine to visit the caves in the morning, catch the lunchtime bus to Itilo via Areopolis, and walk back to the caves.

Start the walk in **Itilo**, a sizeable village, once the centre of a huge slave trade, which has recently lost out to Areopolis as the hub of the deep Mani. There are still cafés lining the central lane in summer, but its narrow alleys and close-packed houses lie quiet and empty. GREEN WALKERS' SIGNS guide you through the village. From the large, paved SQUARE where the bus stops, walk down the road between the square and the café-taverna Η Πετρινη Γωνια. After 20m turn right down a concrete alley (ΚΑΚΤΟΣ); then, after 30m, turn left (ΟΔΟΣ ... ΡΑΖΕΛΟΥ) and go past the TOWN HALL on your left. At a widening with a telephone pole in the middle, turn right down a concrete alley, bending right. You reach a stone-slabbed SITTING AREA (**5min**), also accessible from other parts of the village.

From here, a cobbled path descends steeply, out of the village, with views across the gorge to the large pentagonal perimeter wall of Kelefa Castle (see Car tour 3).

71

You can visit this later, if it tempts you.

Go through the forecourt of the small 13th-century Byzantine chapel of **Sotiros** (**10min**), tucked against the sandstone cliffs. At the larger path, turn sharp left to reach a dirt track (**15min**).

Turn right here, for an out-and-back visit to the ruined monastery and chapel of **Dekoulou** (**22min**). You in fact walk past it before turning sharp left to reach the parking area outside it, where a canine welcoming committee awaits! As the chapel is privately owned, there are no official opening times, but outside school hours (ie after 15.00 in term time) there are usually children in the house next door who can unlock it for you. The church interior is covered from floor to dome in striking frescoes from the 18th century, many of them depicting gruesome martyrdoms, and beautifully lit up in all their earthy and golden hues. The Last Judgement on the west wall is particularly vivid, while the wooden iconostasis (rood screen) is elegantly carved and gilded. Do leave an offering in the candle box. The ruined buildings outside were home to over 150 monks in the 17th century. A secret meeting between the Russian Count Orlov and the Maniot chieftains took place here in 1770, though its outcome — their combined rebellion against the Ottoman Turks — failed.

Return along the dirt track and continue past the place you joined it (**29min**) to a covered SPRING on the left (**31min**). Then continue on the track until it bears left, at which point you can join a path that forks right (**33min**). This short stretch of *kalderimi* is very overgrown in places and some ducking and diving is required to navigate through overhanging branches. (To avoid this over-grown section — which only lasts a few minutes — you *could* continue on from the monastery along the lower road into Itilo and then join the main coastal road at the 40min-point in the walk. There are great views over the bay below, but this detour would add 2.5km to the walk.)

Staying on the *kalderimi*, you pass a house on your left and the path widens (**38min**). Ignore the path on the left and keep straight to join a gravel track. Take the left fork down to the main road (**40min**). Turn left and then right, past the Hotel Porto Vitilo, round to the SEA (**50min**). Here, follow the shore to the left, across a streambed and alongside a stone

Byzantine chapel of Sotiros, below Itilo

wall; it may be easier to walk on the left-hand side of the wall. Beyond a two-storey house (**1h**), you pick up a track, which joins an asphalt road.

*If you want to make a **detour to Kelefá castle**, turn left to the main road and, from south of the Hotel Itilo, take a dirt track zigzagging up the hillside to the ruined fort. Allow 1h30min for the 5km round trip.*

The main walk continues straight ahead along the asphalt road, past a café and into the seaside village of **Neo Itilo** (also called Tsipa). The beach here is sandy, and there are showers to wash off afterwards. At the T-junction in the village (**1h15min**), turn left up to the main road (**1h20min**). Follow this to the right for 100m, curving right. At the end of a long white bungalow on the left (**1h22min**), turn left and immediately right, alongside a wall with a RED WAYMARK, and locate the start of the cobbled mulepath to Areopolis. After a few zigzags and some invasive broom bushes, the path clears up, straightens out and climbs steadily up the rocky hillside, with expanding views over Itilo bay and Limeni village. You go through TWO GATES, after which a newly bulldozed track has in part superseded the *kalderimi*. Pass a farm (and go through another gate; **2h15min**); five minutes later you rejoin the asphalt road. Turn left and, after 30m, turn sharp right on a signposted asphalt road which cuts the hairpin bend and rejoins the road (**2h23min**). Follow the road to the right, and at the junction (**2h30min**) keep right, under a sign welcoming you to **Areopolis**. Keep right/straight on into the village centre. At the junction by the curious twin chapels of **Ayios Haralambos** and **Panayitsa** (**2h37min**), turn left for the modern town square, with its

tavernas, taxi rank and bus station (ticket office in the café).

To continue the walk to the caves, turn right from the twin chapels, down the cobbled lane and into the old part of the village. Keep left in front of the 18th-century CATHEDRAL (**2h40min**), dedicated — as befits the warlike Maniots — to the Taxiarches or Archangels. Opposite its tall and elegant steeple, by Pierros Bozagregos' pension, turn left down ΟΔΟΣ ΤΖΑΝΗ ΤΖΑΝΕΤΑΚΗ, named after a Prime Minister from the Mani. At the junction, keep right, passing a fine TOWER-HOUSE, to reach an asphalt road (**2h45min**). Follow this to the right, passing an optimistic sign to 'DYROS BAY — CAVES BY WALK 3KM'. The lane forks left and passes through fields before starting a gentle descent to the hamlet of Krialianika (marked on maps as Omales). Ahead of you lies the bay of Diros, with the village of Pirgos on the hill behind, and the tall Sklavounakos tower breaking the skyline.

In **Krialianika** (**3h**) ignore the road forking left, signed 'XEPAPA-DIANIKA'. Follow the lane, which soon becomes a dirt track, descending via TWO GATES and a left bend. Ignore the track heading down to the sea and keep straight on, following ORANGE ARROW WAYMARKS, until you emerge on the asphalt road. Turn right to the beach at **Dirós** (**3h37min**). You may spot the plaque commemorating the battle of Diros on 15 June 1826, when 300 local women beat back an invading Turkish navy with their sickles, while their menfolk were defending the front line at Verga (near Kalamata).

At the end of the beach, follow the track left up to a WATERWORKS BUILDING (**3h45min**). Go up to the right of this and, by a square manhole, follow a line of cemented rocks to the right. After 30m, turn left (RED ARROW), climb up a low wall and follow a small path through sage and spurge bushes. Red waymarks guide you through a BLUE GATE (**3h53min**), down some big steps and through a carpet of *Mesembryanthemum* to emerge on the bend of a road just below the **Neolithic Museum** (**3h55min**). The cave ticket office is a few minutes' walk up to your left, while to your right are the café, shop, pebbly beach and the **Pirgos Dirou Sea-caves** (**4h**).

The tour of the main **Vlyhada Cave** system lasts about 25 minutes, with a boatman punting groups of 6-8 visitors around a sinuous 1200m-long watercourse into the bowels of the mountain. It is all wonderfully reminiscent of Charon, the mythical boatman who ferried the souls of the half-dead from the Elysian Fields to Hades, taking payment of one *obol*, while you kept a second under your tongue in case you made it back. Don't worry too much about missing his Greek commentary, which mainly concerns the imaginative names given to passing stalactite formations; though he may periodically remind you to keep your hands inside the boat, and to avoid touching the stalactites or rocking the boat. If you have time to kill until your visit, check out the Neolithic Museum, displaying finds from the adjacent **Alepo-trypa Cave**. This was inhabited by Bronze Age families until an earthquake blocked the entrance around 3000 BC.

After your visit, the BUS leaves from the small parking area outside the cave entrance and souvenir shop.

Walk 12: THREE GRASSY MEADOWS: THALAMES • SOMATIANA • LANGADA • THALAMES

Distance/time: 11km/7mi; 4h
Grade: strenuous with an ascent from 400m/1300ft to 1100m/3600ft, mainly on rocky paths. The initial descent down to the third meadow is steep and overgrown in places as the route passes through dense trees and scrub oak.

Equipment: water, sunhat and sunscreen, pullover, picnic. A walking stick is strongly recommended.
Transport: 🚗 to/from Thalames (Car tour 2 after 191km). Or 🚌 from Kardamyli to Thalames (Timetable 8).

This walk takes you away from the hustle and bustle of tourism on the coast and up into the peace of the mountains, where life has a very different, agricultural flavour. The route runs unexpectedly through three grassy meadows, passing walnut and apple orchards, with the distant sound of goat-bells clanging a constant soundtrack. The only human life you are likely to encounter is the odd shepherd or two. The end of the walk gives a glimpse into life in a Mani village — both Thalames and Langada have a handful of tower houses.

Start the hike from the main square at **Thalames**, with the PLATANOS taverna and olive oil press. Head south on the main road, but turn left immediately up an unsigned concrete road. This leads to the hamlet of **Somatiana** (8min).
The concrete road becomes a dirt track, drops down a little and then starts to climb. Leave this road at a sharp right-hand bend (17min): head up to the left, at the left side

of a clearly definable gulley. This path soon becomes a rough *kalderimi*. Your walk will encircle the hill to your right.
Keep to the left of the streambed. After you have passed a DRYSTONE WALL running parallel to the path (27min), drop down into the streambed and continue steeply up the other side. Soon you pass a STONE ENCLOSURE used for livestock, and you may notice quite a few engravings on rocks in

Stone watering troughs in the first, small meadow

this area — nothing of anthropological interest, just bored shepherds entertaining themselves…

The path becomes a little clearer as you come to another STONE HUT and regain the dirt road you left at the 17min-point. Ignore the left fork leading down to a farm holding. A small church, **Agios Vasilios** (**52min**), is the next landmark on the right, but it's not very interesting as it was only built in 1959 and has no wall paintings inside.

Some 150m past the church, the road bends sharply left. At this point you should head off the road onto a rocky path heading up the left side of another gulley (**55min**). The path criss-crosses the streambed and emerges on the FIRST, SMALL MEADOW (**1h15min**). Head straight across towards a GROUP OF WALNUT TREES. The path begins again to the left of a large CISTERN and STONE WATERING TROUGHS. It climbs steadily, rising to a much LARGER GRASSY MEADOW (**1h35min**). Once on the plateau, bear right and head towards the HUT at the far end, which makes a perfect place to stop for lunch.

Hut in the second, larger meadow

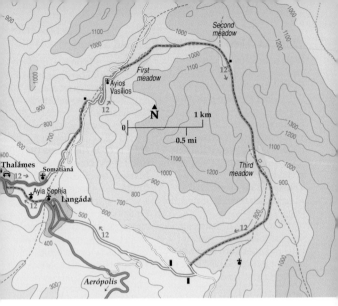

From the hut keep going in the same direction, locating the path that begins in the floor of the next gulley. This takes you up to the TREE-LINED SADDLE visible ahead. Pass to the right of a rocky outcrop and then another GROUP OF WALNUT TREES (**1h50min**). Keep to the left of the next outcrop and head towards a DERELICT STONE ANIMAL ENCLOSURE (**2h**).

Just beyond this your descent begins, initially down the right side of the valley. The third meadow is soon visible below, enabling you to to get your bearings: you will turn right down the final valley from the centre of this third meadow. The path is initially quite steep, and a dense wood of oak trees makes it difficult to follow in places (as a general rule, keep within sight of the thin black water pipe). Once out of the woods, the path becomes a little clearer, winding down through scrub oak to the apple orchard below, where you keep to the right of the trees.

Once past the ORCHARD (**2h40min**), identify the circular concrete lid of another cavernous WATER CISTERN (and take a peek inside). To the right of this is a low wall in a break in the tree line. Hop over the wall, to find your rocky path downhill starting on the left and then swinging over to the right.

At the CONCRETE ROAD (**3h15min**) turn left and then almost immediately right, to pass a RUINED TOWER. Ten minutes later, at the T-junction (**3h25min**), turn right and follow this track all the way into the village of Langada. As you enter **Langada** (**3h 42min**), ignore the right turn by the house with the green door and carry on downhill. At the next junction, with blue doors, turn right and then, after only 20m, go left down some steps. At the bottom of the steps turn right down an alley. Soon you will come to some steps that take you down to the main road. Turn right into the VILLAGE SQUARE, pass the CHURCH and follow the GREEN WALKERS' SIGN along a great *kalderimi*, passing the restored church of **Agia Sophia** en route. When you emerge on the main road, turn right, back to the main square in **Thalames** (**4h**).

Walk 13: TWO SHORT WALKS NEAR STAVRI

Walk a: Odigitria Chapel
Distance/time: 2km/1.2mi; 1h
Grade: easy, but you must be sure-footed and have a head for heights
Equipment: water, sunhat, sunscreen, torch. A walking stick is useful for the rocky terrain, long sleeves/trousers for the overgrown stretches.
Transport: 🚍 to/from Ayia Kyriaki, 1km north of Stavri village (Car tour 3 at 34km). In Stavri, follow the road to the right (past the hotel on your right), ignore the left turn to Kipoula, and leave the village. Ignore a small left fork to

Χαραμπος (Harambos). Park where the road bends right to climb into the hamlet of Ayia Kyriaki. 🚍 Areopolis–Stavri–Gerolimenas line (Timetable 20). Alight in Stavri and walk to Ayia Kyriaki (2km; 30min return).

Walk b: Cape Tigani and the castle of the Grande Magne
Distance/time: 5km/3mi; 2h
Grade: easy, though the peninsula is very rough and rocky
Equipment: water, sunscreen, sunhat; jacket (if windy); a stick is useful for the very rocky terrain; long trousers for the nettles.
Transport: as Walk a above

If you only have time for one short walk in the whole of the Mani, head for the delightful little chapel of Odigitria, set at the foot of a cliff overlooking the sparkling sea. Its setting is spectacular, the peace almost guaranteed, and the adjacent caves a reminder of the pains hermits took to find solitude.

If you have more time and energy, and enjoy piecing historic forts together in your mind, hike out to the rocky, sea-swept spit of the Tigani (Frying-pan). On its very tip perch the low ruins of a huge Frankish castle, probably the 'Grande Magne' which gave the Mani its name. Debate still rages as to whether or not this is the 'awesome crag on a promontory' where in 1249 the Frankish prince, Guillaume de Villehardouin 'built a castle and named it Maine' (Chronicle of the Morea). It is certainly the most likely candidate, providing a sheltered anchorage, unscalable sea cliffs and a sizeable surface area, but the inhabitants of Kelefa and Porto Kayio may claim that their castle is the one. Not much remains here, but it is still a fine, bracing walk to a sea-swept site.

Start Walk a from below Ayia Kyriaki: walk straight on (north) along a paved track, and through a blue METAL GATE (**2min**). A decaying walkers' sign refers to PANAYIA AGITRIA (Virgin Mary the 'holy three'), a twisted version of Odigitria (The Guide). No doubt her guidance was often called upon to reach this elusive chapel. After 10 minutes along what has become a dirt track, the well-camouflaged church appears on

your left, at the foot of a cliff. Where the track ends (**22min**), pick up a narrow path that runs between some rocks and descends a steep ledge beside stone side-walls (vertigo is a possibility here), then contours southwest through high bushes. Soon you reach the small 13th-century cruciform chapel of **Odigitria** (**30min**), which is always open. Inside are carved columns, a marble iconostasis, and darkening frescoes

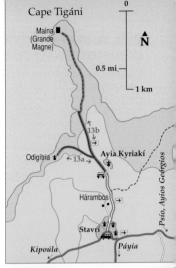

of the Archangels. Behind the chapel are three carved-out caves where presumably hermits once lived — you can make out a cistern, some niches and perhaps a bread oven.

Return the way you came to **Ayia Kyriaki** (**1h**).

Start Walk b by following Walk a to the **4min**-point, then keep straight ahead. The concrete dwindles to a stony track. You pass the village CEMETERY on your right (**5min**), after which the track deteriorates further, before finally petering out near a high sea-cliff (**12min**). Continue along a small path which bears right, passing a STONE HUT — a good landmark for your return.

At the bottom of the slope (**20min**), you need to cross the pathless, barren 'handle' of the 'frying-pan' peninsula, making for the right-hand corner of the ruined castle, where the defence wall is most visible. You pass hand-cut SALT PANS and stone huts where, until the 1960s, salt-collectors worked for days in blistering heat, loading mules with sea-salt to be sold onto the ferry in Mezapos. Small CAIRNS here and there help you find the smoothest way among the mess of boulders. Jagged rocks and sea-urchins make it difficult to get into the sea for a swim — the easiest places are on the left side.

Finally you enter the castle of the **Grande Magne** (**40min**) through its original gateway, at the eastern end of the landward wall. In front of you are the remains of a basilica, with some fallen columns and carved tie-beams, which suggest it was built before the Franks. The whole place seems to have been abandoned in the 17th century because of rampant piracy. You can follow the 750 metres of crumbling, nettle-covered perimeter wall around the tip of the headland, past towers

Photograph: the door of Odigitria

and turrets, and back again. It is from these sea cliffs that, according to a medieval ballad, the black knight Mavroeidis and his captured princess, both sitting astride his trusty white stallion, leapt into the foaming sea and were carried to safety by the formidable steed. If you wander around the interior, watch out for collapsed WATER CISTERNS.

Return to the main gateway (**1h**) and follow the same route back to **Ayia Kyriaki** (**2h**).

Walk 14: GEROLIMENAS • PEPON • LEONTAKIS • (MOUNTANISTIKA) • GEROLIMENAS

See also photograph page 21
Distance/time: 9.5km/6mi; 3h 30min (plus up to 50min detours)
Grade: moderate, with 550m/1800ft of steady ascent on tracks and paths
Equipment: water, sunhat and sunscreen, picnic, jumper for windy Mountanistika. A walking stick is useful for the rocky terrain, and long sleeves/trousers for the overgrown stretches. If you want to see inside Ayios Stratigos chapel, make prior arrangements with the warden (see Car tour 3, box page 21), and take a torch.
Transport: 🚗 to/from Gerolimenas (Car tour 3 at 43km). 🚐 Areopolis to/from Gerolimenas (Timetables 20, 21).

This circular walk gives you a taste of the tower villages which lurk in the barren, rocky folds of the Mani mountains, without the logistical hassle of crossing the spine completely and having to find transport back. The hidden hamlet of Pepon, the sentinel towers of Leontakis and the 'bristling ridge' of Mountanistika are three of the most impressive fortified settlements.

Start the walk at the seafront HOTEL AKROYIALI in **Gerolimenas**: follow the road inland, back towards AREOPOLIS, ignoring the left fork to 'Post' (if the post office still exists by the time you read this). After 80m, turn right up a concrete road with the faded name ΟΔΟΣ ... ΜΑΝΤΟΥΒΑΛΟΥ (and, from the other direction, a sign to Ano Boularii). Cross straight over the Areopolis–Alika road (**6min**), up a concrete road.
At the first house of **Ano Boularii** (**27min**), keep right/straight and, by a large TOWER (**30min**) keep

left. The concrete climbs past a modern mauve-brown CHURCH and crosses a dry gully on a BRIDGE. Just after this there is a wall on your left. If you like old churches, take a detour here.

Detour to Ayios Panteleïmon chapel (20min return): Follow the top of the wall north for about 500m, and where it stops, keep going, looking left, to unearth a low stone-slate chapel nestling in the olive groves. It is one of the oldest in Greece (991 AD), with an unusual double apse and striking frescoes.

Gerolimenas

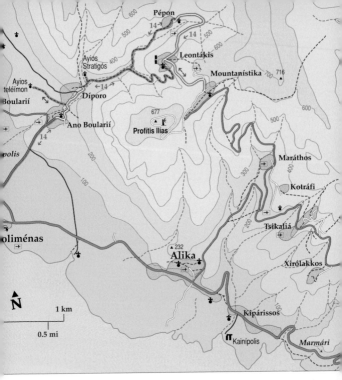

The main walk keeps straight ahead from the bridge: follow the steepening concrete lane up past the Mantouvalos Tower to where it ends by the uppermost houses of **Díporo**. Continue straight up a jeep track for 20m, then turn right on a path marked with red dots. This passes between a street lamp and a well-maintained TOWER-HOUSE (**40min**), where you can make a second detour.

Detour to Ayios Stratigos chapel (5min return): From this house a path leads left to the low stone chapel of the 'Holy General' — the Archangel Michael, shown on page 21. If you have got hold of the warden, you can marvel at an almost complete cycle of 12th-century frescoes coming to life in your torch beams. If not you can sit and admire its simple, curved lines, with pretty dentil-course and tiled arches.

The main walk continues by following the path down into the

dry STREAMBED (**43min**) and up the other side. After a couple of zigzags it heads steadily up the south bank of the valley, keeping a stone's throw above the bed. You can see the twin towers of Leontakis keeping watch from the top of a rounded summit ahead. At the JUNCTION OF GULLIES (**1h10min**), the path dips to cross the right-hand gully and heads up the left one. You pass a roofless CISTERN, and short cut a zigzag. You soon cross this overgrown gully, then dip briefly back into it before resuming along the north bank.

The first dry-stone wall crossing the path has conveniently crumbled — so continue straight ahead following occasional RED WAYMARKS. Turn left and clamber up to **Pepon** — to a house with a balcony. Here turn right, past a telephone pole and several ruined houses, before dropping down to the lane (**1h45min**). This loops

81

Above: flower-filled track between Pepon and Leontakis

steadily uphill to the equally deserted village of **Leontakis** (**2h05min**), where those seemingly inaccessible towers rise just to your right. From here the lane continues through a second loop to reach the bristling skyline of Mountanistika.

Detour to Mountanistika (30min return): *The detour to this impregnable settlement, numbering over 50 tower houses strung along a windy 550m-high ridge, epitomises the fierce and indomitable spirit of the Mani. It is also susceptible to the rolling sea-mist which locals call* kotsifari (*dark as a blackbird*), *so hopefully you have come prepared.*

There is no café, only an unreliable cardphone — and you are unlikely to meet any of its inhabitants.

The main walk turns back from Leontakis. Head left towards the very visible MAIN CHURCH. Just after the church, a WALKERS' SIGN on your left indicates a narrow, walled-in path on the right. You pass a SMALL STONE CHAPEL (**2h35min**) and follow the path down the south side of the Leontakis hill. When you rejoin your outgoing path (**2h50min**), turn left and retrace your steps through **Diporo** and **Ano Boulari**, back to **Gerolimenas** (**3h30min**).

Walk 15: PALIROS • VATHY BAY • KOKKINOYIA • TEMPLE OF POSEIDON • CAPE TAINARON • KOKKINOYIA

Distance/time: 10km/6.2mi; 3h15min
Grade: moderate, with no huge climbs or descents. Most of the outward route follows concrete tracks (with one short steep stretch across rocky hillsides), most of the return a little-used lane.
Equipment: sunhat, sunscreen, picnic, water. Jacket if windy. Sandals if you plan to swim (lots of sea-urchins). Walking stick and long trousers useful on the one short rocky, overgrown stretch

Transport: 🚌 to/from the Paliros turn-off (Car tour 3 just after 57km). 🚐 Areopolis to Gerolimenas or Alika (Timetable 20) and taxi from there, or 🚐 to the Marmari junction (Timetable 20) and walk (just 1km).
Short walk: Kokkinoyia — Cape Tainaron — Kokkinoyia. 4.2km/2.6mi; 1h30min; easy. 🚌 to/from **Kokkinoyia** (Car tour 3 at 60km). Follow the main walk from the 1h35min-point to the cape and return the same way.

You would never guess that the tip of this barren and rocky peninsula, the southernmost point of mainland Greece, has seen civilisations rise and fall. The classical Greeks built a city around a temple to Poseidon 'of Tainaron'. In Roman times, its azure inlets sheltered merchant fleets, trading with the 'Free Laconians'. For the Crusaders, it was one of the last chances to pick up Christian mercenaries en route to the Holy Land. Now it is the site of a lonely lighthouse blinking across the endless seas at Crete and northern Africa. Reaching Cape Tainaron (or Matapan) used to mean quite a hike, but a recently-paved road as far as the temple of Poseidon at Kokkinoyia leaves only a 2km walk to the lighthouse. But if you start and end near the tower settlement of Paliros and the deep fjord-like inlet of Vathy, you'll have a lovely half-day circuit.

Start the walk from the layby on the east side of the **road to Cape Tainaron**, just 50m south of the turn-off to Miánes. Retrace the road for 150m, back to the junction signposted to 'PALIROS' and turn right on the concrete road. At an unsignposted Y-fork after 400m, go right (**5min**). The main part of **Paliros**, a fortified stone-built village with a handful of elderly occupants, lies up to your left.
The track descends a south-facing spur to the isolated houses of **Koureli**. At the end of the track, by a small CHURCH (**23min**), continue straight on along a walled path between the houses.

After 150m, by a telephone pole (**25min**), turn right down a walled path (sign to 'BEACH', and blue paint spot). This descends steadily to some umbrella pines in the valley floor. Keep left to reach the pebbly beach of **Vathy** (**35min**), set deep in its sheltered inlet and tempting for a swim even in winter.
From the far (southern) end of the beach (**40min**), turn inland up a gully, keeping on the left side, a few metres above the bottom (BLUE SPOTS). After 100m, follow the BLUE ARROWS steeply up scrubby hillsides, along a semblance of a path on the left (true right) slope of the gully. You

may disturb wild quail (which gave their name to Porto Kayio) or spot migrating bee-eaters stocking up for their long sea-flight. At a STONE WALL (**55min**), cross the gully (blue spot) and, after 50m, bear right (uphill), parallel to a low stone wall. Climb a rocky bank to the PAVED ROAD (**1h05min**) and turn left. The road descends past the scattered modern houses of **Kokkinoyia**, the last of which has a year-round café, to end in front of the chapel of **Ayii Asomati** (Bodiless Saints, ie archangels; **1h15min**).

You are now standing in the ancient city of **Tainaron**, which was a major hub of the Union of Free Laconians. This league of 20 cities, put together by the Romans to counter Spartan might, boasted its own coinage, dialect and worship. From the church, a path leads left down to a turquoise bay, which was the location of a temple and **sanctuary to Poseidon**. Square-hewn blocks from its base have been incorporated into the Asomati chapel. Behind this bay is a small cave, used now to shelter fishing boats, which has been

The well-preserved circular mosaic at the Poseidon sanctuary at Tainaron

Nearby Porto Kayio, with the village and fort of Achilleio behind the beach

suggested as the entrance to Hades (the Underworld) used by Hercules to catch the three-headed guard dog Cerberus. But the cave does not appear to be very deep. There are other entrances to Hades dotted around Greece, used by Orpheus, Theseus and (at the Styx on Mt Helmos) by the dead.

Back at Ayii Asomati (**1h25min**), continue along the path descending to the cove on the right. You pass some CISTERNS hewn out of the living rock in a delicate amphora shape. These gave the site its local name of **Sternes**. Little channels on the surface, which collected rainwater, are still visible. After the cove the path passes more square-hewn cuttings before passing near a well-preserved CIRCULAR MOSAIC with wave patterns. Two better-preserved CISTERNS, one of which has a fig tree growing out of it, lie off to your left.

The path continues around a THIRD COVE (**1h35min**) and, shadowed by derelict telephone poles, up a rocky slope. Cistus, *Crupina* and occasional orchids bloom here in spring, while blue rock thrush shimmer among the boulders. After 20 minutes you join the rocky spine, and follow the path down to the LIGHTHOUSE at **Cape Tainaron** (**2h05min**). The sizeable building, which once housed a keeper and his family, is deserted and its operation has been automated. At 36.4° latitude, you are further south than Tunis and Algiers, and only marginally further north than Tarifa, mainland Europe's southernmost point. Tankers ply past in both directions with a faint rumble. There is no drinking water, little shade and frequent wind, so hopefully you have come prepared.

Return the same way to **Kokkinoyia** (**2h40min**), and follow the road, heading north, all the way back to your car or pre-arranged taxi at the layby just before the junction with the PALIROS ROAD (**3h15min**). Or walk on to the bus stop at the Marmari junction.

85

Walk 16: KOUMOUSTA • GHOLAS MONASTERY • RASINA VALLEY • KOUMOUSTA

Distance/time: 13.4km/8.3mi; 3h45min

Grade: fairly easy — most of the 350m/1150ft ascent is on a lovely path in the shade.

Equipment: water, sunhat and sunscreen, picnic. A walking stick is useful for the rocky terrain, and long sleeves/trousers for the overgrown stretches.

Transport: 🚗 to/from Koumousta (a detour from Xirokambi, the 115km-point in Car tour 2). Keep right, to the upper part of the village, and park by the paved square with plane tree. There is also a 🚐 from Sparta to Xirokambi (Timetable 24), from where you could walk to Koumousta and join the walk at the 17min-point (turning left), but this adds 10km return!

Shorter walk: Koumousta — Gholas Monastery — Koumousta. 6.4km/4mi; 2h15min; grade as main walk. Follow the main walk to the monastery and return the same way.

The secret village of Koumousta is completely hidden in a deep fold of Mt Taygetus' eastern foothills. Its road link to Xirokambi town, snaking through the Rasina Gorge, was only completed in 1990. Most of the 50 or so houses now lie empty, although a few are being restored, and one is available as a simple hostel for rent. Historically, it was the winter quarters for farmers summering in the high meadows of Pendavli, and is marked on many maps as Pendavli. This walk starts and ends in Koumousta, following a path up to the 17th-century monastery of Gholas, a gravel jeep track along a spur of the mountain, and a dirt road back down again.

Start the walk from the paved square in the *pano hora* (upper village) of **Koumousta**, with its huge plane tree and gushing six-spouted spring. Follow the paved lane left (south), as indicated by the panel (*'GHOLA MONASTERY 1H'*) and 'Japanese-flag' waymarks. The paving stops; follow the dirt track past crumbling houses and out of the village, towards the towering cliffs of Stefani opposite. Just right of these cliffs is a narrow valley, up which you will be walking. After a right bend (**4min**), fork left, and fork left again after a short uphill stretch (**10min**). At a SIGNPOST (**15min**), turn sharp left along a larger track and, after 100m (**17min**) turn sharp right down a

Gholas Monastery

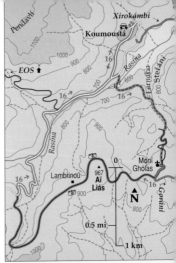

signed path. After 80m, turn sharp left into some oak woods, then sharp right and across a loose LOG BRIDGE over a seasonal trickle. Soon you cross a more substantial stream on an arched STONE BRIDGE (**22min**), screened by a canopy of plane trees. The path climbs left past some boulders, then bears right into the **Larnakia Valley**, tunnelling through the thick kermes oaks. Cross a WOODEN BRIDGE over the (usually dry) gully on your left (**45min**), and five minutes later a SECOND FOOT-BRIDGE across a side gully, bearing right. At the jeep track (**55min**), keep left, climbing steadily. Just after a right bend (**1h**), fork left up a stepped path, cross the track again, and continue up through chestnut woods. Then bear left to the track which leads up to **Gholas Monastery** (**1h10min**).

Founded in 1632, the monastery once numbered over 50 monks — hence its size — but like almost all Greek monasteries suffered from 'pagan drift' in the last century. After the death of the last nun, the monastery was resettled in 2000 by three young monks from Ayios Ioannis on Evia (Euboea). During daylight hours, and so long as you are decently dressed and refrain from smoking and taking photos, they will show you through the well-tended courtyard to the central chapel, covered in frescoes by the 17th-century iconographer Dimitrios Kakavas. It is dedicated to Zoodochou Pigis (Virgin Mary the Spring of Life), celebrated on the Friday after (Orthodox) Easter.

From the monastery follow the asphalt road uphill for 500m, to a junction at a left bend (**1h18min**). Here turn right along a dirt track. Ignore small tracks left and right, and continue uphill, passing to the north of the 967m hump of **Aï Lias**. After 2km you pass the *mandri* (sheep barn) of **Lambri-**

The flower-filled jeep track

nou (**1h50min**), and earn fine views south to the peaks of Zizali and the Laconian Sea. Another 800m sees you crossing the 980m RIDGE (**2h**) at the walk's highest point and looping around the head of a forested valley on the little-used, flower-covered jeep track shown above. This descends to a junction with a larger dirt track (**2h35min**), where you turn right. The track winds down to the floor of the **Rasina Valley**, crosses the main stream (**3h**) and is joined by a track coming down from the EOS refuge (Walk 17). Opposite a vertical crag on the right bank (**3h20min**), a path leads to a lovely spot by the water's edge. Continue downstream along the main track, then climb slightly to a fork (**3h30min**), where you turn left and follow your outgoing track into **Koumousta** (**3h45min**).

Walk 17: ASCENT OF MT TAYGETUS: PROFITIS ILIAS (AÏ LIAS) PEAK

Distance/time: 9km/5.6mi; 6h
Grade: strenuous, with 900m/2950ft of steady (sometimes steep) climb and descent over rough, rocky terrain. No shade. Without special equipment, the ascent is only feasible from May to October, and even during these months be prepared for sudden storms and low temperatures, as well as soft snow patches outside high summer. You should not attempt this hike without some previous experience of high-mountain walking — you are further from civilisation than on any other walk in this book. Having made those provisos, the path itself is well marked with an assortment of paint spots and posts, mostly red or red-on-white ('32'). It is rarely very steep, apart from about 10 minutes at the start/end. And you may well meet other hikers en route, offering advice or encouragement!
Equipment: plenty of water, picnic, sunhat, sunglasses, sunscreen including lip protection, wind- and waterproof jacket, warm jumper or fleece, compass, torch. A walking stick is extremely useful for the rocky terrain.
Transport: 🚐 (preferably 4WD) to/from the refuge of Ayia Varvara, a 15km detour from Paleopanayia (Car tour 2 at 112.5km). From Paleopanayia follow the surfaced road past Toriza and Krioneri (Poliana) to the junction below Manganiari Spring (8.6km). Here, turn left up an unsurfaced track; you may see orange and red waymarks, after the second left-hand hairpin bend, indicating a path to the refuge. After 4.3km, fork right ('EOS Refuge') up a rough track — this may be impassable for low cars, or for any vehicle before late May. Keep right in front of the shepherd's hut on a small plateau, and park in front of the refuge, 2.1km further on. (To book the refuge, which contains 26 bunks, blankets, kitchen, stove and water tank, contact EOS Spartis on 27310 22574 or at 97 Gortsologou St, Sparta (evenings only); bear in mind that the warden's fixed fee makes it expensive for small groups.)

This is the classic ascent of Taygetus, starting from an unstaffed mountain refuge at Ayia Varvara (1550m altitude) and following the well-marked trail all the way to the pyramidal 2400m peak and back again. It goes without saying that the views from the top are fabulous, and ample reward for the stiff climb. The limestone and schist slopes are bleak and lunar, but, on closer inspection, reveal interesting rocks and crystals, as well as hardy alpine flowers and shrubs (best in May and June).

Start the walk at **Ayia Varvara**. (The refuge is usually locked, and its only public water source is a spring five minutes' walk down the northern slope.) Follow the path west, then bending northwest past the last of those magnificent black pines. At the gully (**5min**), the path climbs steeply for about 10 minutes (it is best to head right then left), before resuming a steadier gradient towards the outlying peak of Vassiliko Vouno (Royal Mountain). At around 1700m in altitude (**30min**), there is another small grassy plateau, and again at 1820m (**1h**) a larger one with a huge hollow to your left (an area called **Gouves**). Just after this the path makes an important left bend and traverses southwest, with the occasional steeper zigzag.

Eventually (**1h30min**) you find yourself walking up one of the slanting limestone *zonaria* (strata) which point towards the summit. A last right turn brings you out on the 2250m saddle called **Portes** (**2h15min**) — this is a generic term and not to be confused with the 'Portes' 5km north along the same ridge.

From here, with the rounded bulk of **Athanati Rahi** (Ridge) to your right (north), turn left (south) keeping just to the right of the ridge. At a natural SINKHOLE (**2h25min**), veer right and follow the clear lines etched in the loose, slabby rubble of Profitis Ilias' northern face. Where the path

Snow-covered slopes of Profitis Ilias in November

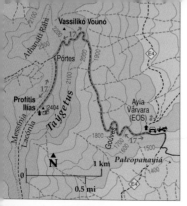

Goats enjoying the view north along the Pendadhactilo Ridge from Athanati Ridge (Athanati Rahi)

splits and rejoins, I always recommend taking the longer, gentler option. Finally, you crest the summit of **Profitis Ilias** (**3h15min**; 2407m — or 2404m or 2411m, depending on which map you have), the highest point in the Peloponnese. There is a roofless stone chapel dedicated to the Prophet Elijah, where hundreds of people from both sides of the mountain congregate on the 19th July every year for a moonlit mass, followed by music and feasts — and prayers that the weather holds! If it doesn't they cram into the two tiny stone huts alongside. Many Greek mountaintops bear the name of Elijah, not because the prophet was taken up to heaven from a high place, but because, in the Christianisation of pagan names, mountaintop shrines to Ilios (sun) transmuted most easily into Ilias

(Elijah). Likewise, chapels dedicated to Ayios Nikolaos are often on the site of temples to Poseidon, churches of Ayia Sofia where Athena was worshipped, and so on.

If you have good weather, the peak is a marvellous place to rest your aching legs, with views west down to Kardamyli and the Messinian coast, east over Sparta and the Laconian plain and gulf, south to the rugged peaks of Zizali, and southeast over Kythira (on a clear day) to the faint nipples of Crete's White Mountains, suspended over a misty sea. You may see the triangular shadow of the peak projected onto the plain (or clouds) below you — a mesmerising sight. The jagged limestone spine to your north is often called the *'pendadhactilo'* (five-fingered) — legend has it that Jesus used the ridge as a giant hand-hold when climbing up to heaven, leaving five massive finger imprints. From north to south, and in approximately descending order of height, these splendidly-named peaks are: Profitis Ilias, Athanati Rahi (Immortal Ridge), Sidhirokastro (Iron Castle), Marmarokastro (Marble Castle) and — after a gap — Spanakaki (Little Spinach — after, I suppose, a wild green which grows on its lower flanks). Talking of plants, you are welcome to pick some of the much-prized mountain tea (see page 101, after the 2h07min-point) sprouting between rocks on the higher slopes of Taygetus. You may also spot spring crocus or autumn snowdrops among the deceptively prickly shrubs, and sleek black choughs wheeling showily overhead.

Do leave enough time and energy for the joint-jarring descent to the **Ayia Varvara** refuge (**6h**), and for the drive back to civilisation.

Walk 18: AYIOS GEORGIOS CHAPEL • ANAVRITI • SOHA • KALIVIA SOHAS

See also photograph page 15
Distance/time: 13km/8mi; 4h45min
Grade: moderate, with an ascent of 400m/1300ft on a well-graded mulepath to Anavriti and a flattish dirt road to Soha. 500m/1640ft descent on a partly-cobbled path to Kalivia, initially flat, then winding unremittingly downhill. This path, though broad and regularly used, demands a head for heights.
Equipment: water, sunhat and sunscreen, picnic. A walking stick is useful for the rocky terrain, and long sleeves/trousers for the overgrown stretches.

Transport: 🚌 to/from Ayios Georgios Chapel (detour from Parori, the 94.8-point in Car tour 2). Return from Kalivia to Ayios Georgios by taxi (many in Sparta). If necessary, show this to the taxi driver: το εκκλησακι του Αγιου Γεωργιου στο δρομο για την Αναβρυτη, εκει που ξεκιναει το παλιο καλντεριμι. 🚌 Sparta–Anavriti (Timetable 25); alight at Ayios Georgios; as there is no official stop, use the phrase for taxi drivers above. Return by 🚌 (Kalivia–Sparta, Timetable 23).

Alternative walk: Ayios Georgios — Anavriti — Faneromeni Monastery — Langadiotissa Gorge — Parori. 9.6km/6mi; 3h30min; fairly easy. *If you only have one day in the area, this combines the best of Walks 18 and 19.* It starts with the lovely mulepath ascent to Anavriti (Walk 18), follows the well-signed E4 footpath to Faneromeni, and descends the dramatic Langadiotissa Gorge to Parori (Walk 19). Transport: It is best to park in Parori and take a taxi (one in Mystras, many in Sparta) to the trailhead — or walk, shortcutting right (southeast) from the *exohiko kendro* (country taverna) of Kefalari along tracks through olive groves to the

Anavriti road (map page 96). First follow the main walk below to Anavriti. Then make for Fanero-meni: follow the road to the right, through the northern *mahalas* (constituent hamlet), after which an E4 signpost indicates the path with black and yellow waymarks. Allow 30-40 minutes to the monastery. Once there, pick up Walk 19 at the 3h50min-point and follow it to Parori.

I f the eastern Taygetus foothills don't make you want to lace up your hiking boots, throw a picnic into a rucksack and hike off through dramatic river gorges to the flower-carpeted meadows and snow-capped peaks, then nothing will! This walk takes you up to two pretty mountain villages perched below the Pendadhactilo Ridge, using old mulepaths for the ascent and descent, with a dirt track in between.

Start the walk at Ayios Georgios: follow the walkers' map and signpost 'ANAVRITI 1H' and red square waymarks up a paved path, climbing steadily. Soon you are following the old *kalderimi* (paved mulepath) which heads west into the **Aeras Ravine**, with orange-grey cliffs opposite. Look back for wonderful views over the Evrotas Plain and the villages around Sparta. A couple of zigzags take you past a metal SHRINE (**25min**), shortly after which the gradient eases and the vegetation becomes lusher. The clear path veers southwest, with the high peaks of Taygetus, snow-capped until May, forming a dramatic backdrop. When you join a lane (**1h**), follow it up to the asphalt road, where you turn right. You soon pass, on the right, the old village SCHOOL, which now houses a geological-botanical exhibition. Continue to the square of **Anavriti** (**1h06min**), with the hotel on your left and cafés ahead — where you may find

the *proedros* (mayor), Thodoris Plevritis, who holds the keys to the exhibition. (As he resides in Sparti, if he is not there ask at the *kafenion*.) Anavriti is the only village on eastern Taygetus with a permanent population. In the 19th century it boasted a flourishing leather industry, with tanneries watered by the powerful springs, and shoemakers' workshops alongside. There was also a limekiln, a tile factory, a silk *fabrica*, an acorn mill (for making tannic dye) and a chandlery. 3000 people (and 20,000 goats and sheep) lived here; now only a few dozen remain, mostly elderly shepherds and returned diaspora from the US.

To continue the main walk to Soha and Kalivia, carry straight on along the lane between the cafés. Follow the main lane (ΤΑΥΓΕΤΟΥ) to the left, past a FOUR-SPOUTED SPRING. Walk downhill, past the last, crumbling houses of the village, to a stream (**1h20min**). The track, now unsurfaced, passes

beneath a pretty clutch of houses called **Kalamareïka**, after the family who settled there (Kalamaras is still the predominant surname in the village). After 1km the track crosses another stream (**1h36min**) near some walnut-shaded meadows. Leaving the north side of the valley, it curves to the right into open, scrub-covered hillsides and, after another 2km, Soha village appears ahead. Then, at a right bend, look out for an IRON CROSS on a rock on your left — one of four protecting the village limits from hail and lightning. Some 50m further on (**2h05min**), take a tiny path scrambling down the stony bank. This is a short cut to Soha church, visible on a spur opposite (the dirt track will also take you there if the path looks tricky). Follow the tiny path, keeping left, to a concrete WATER RESERVOIR (**2h08min**). Here, slightly overgrown, it winds down steadily to the northernmost houses of **Soha** (Pera Mahalas or Korineïka). Pass to the left of a well-maintained house (**2h15min**), keep straight on down some wooden steps, and then fork right. The path crosses the stream which bisects the village (another WOODEN-PLANK BRIDGE) and bears left to climb back to the dirt road (**2h25min**). Follow this left to Soha church (**Presentation of the Virgin**; **2h27min**) which, though locked, has a covered arcade. Around the cobbled square you will find a water-tap, a cardphone and a simple little hostel (unstaffed; key from Vassilis Georgiadis in Sparta; see page 16). From here the route is marked with BLUE SQUARES (some of which have dropped off their wooden posts). Start along the jeep track heading northeast, ignoring a small left fork. The

The path from Soha to Kalivia Sohas

*Jerusalem sage
(Phlomis fruticosa) near Soha*

track then descends gently, bordered by *Crepis rubra* (hawksbeard), *Tordyllium apulum* (a white umbellifer), scabious, poppies and vetch. Oak trees (full-sized, rather than the prickly 'kermes oak' shrub) offer intermittent shade. In front of a gate and VINEYARD (**2h50min**), fork right down a path (WAYMARK) into fields of Jerusalem sage, dotted with yellow asphodels and prickly scrub. The path forks and rejoins, bends right between two oak trees, then winds gently down — you can choose between the roughly paved route or the goats' short cuts. Where the paved path gets overgrown (**3h05min**), hop left onto a clear, marked path.

Detour (50min return): At this point there is also a very scratchy route — 'path' would be a euphemism — diverging right, up the middle of the spur, to its summit. As suggested by the bands of loose rock on the slope, and the unassailable position on top, there was once a fortress (Kastro) here. It had a perimeter wall bridging the spur, two large cisterns and numerous outbuildings.

Continuing on the marked trail, a SHRINE signals the start of the potentially vertiginous stretch — a broad, flagstoned mulepath traversing across a steep rocky slope, with plunging views left over the Retsa Ravine. Vertiginous or not, it is a spectacular feat of drystone
94

engineering. A short climb brings you to a bend (**3h40min**), with the olive- and citrus-studded Evrotas Plain stretching out before you to the foothills of Mt Parnon. Some gently sloping slabs on your left seem made for a view-stop. The path, still paved but less broad, now zigzags mercilessly downhill for 45 minutes. There is one SHRINE — plus, of course, numerous pauses to check on the view — to punctuate the descent. Eventually (**4h25min**) you reach a medieval WATCHTOWER overlooking the gorge to the south; the walls are liable to crumble if clambered on. Bear left towards the red rooves of Kalivia and, at the SIGNPOST (**4h30min**) turn right along a newly paved path to the late 19th-century chapel of **Zoodochou Pigis** (**4h35min**). Go round to its right to reach the *avli* (forecourt), with stone benches and a spring set beneath tall plane trees. The paved path winds down to the first house of **Kalivia Sohas** (**4h40min**), in front of which you can turn left for the centre and simple café (usually open; telephone); or turn right, then left, to reach the road by a 'playground' (**4h45min**). Kalivia ('Huts') was historically the winter quarters for the inhabitants of Soha, and, though more permanent now, is hardly worth lingering in. The BUS STOP is 100m to the left, along the road.

Walk 19: MYSTRAS • TAYGETI • ZOODOCHOU PIGIS MONASTERY • PERGANDEÏKA • FANEROMENI MONASTERY • LANGADIOTISSA GORGE • MYSTRAS

See also photos pages 13, 15
Distance/time: 14.5km/9mi; 5h30min
Grade: moderate, with a steady initial ascent of 800m/2625ft and a steeper onward path through the valley of Pergandeïka (300m/1000ft descent, 100m/330ft ascent) to Faneromeni. After this, the going improves for the final descent of 600m/1970ft (although for the Langadiotissa Gorge descent you must have a head for heights).
Equipment: water, sunhat and sunscreen, picnic. A walking stick is useful for the rocky terrain, as are long sleeves/trousers for the overgrown stretches.
Transport: 🚗 to/from Mystras village (Car tour 2 at 93.8km). 🚌 or taxi: from Sparta, there are hourly buses from a smaller station off Kon. Palaiologou St, a few blocks west of the central square (Timetable 26); though a taxi is easier and hardly more expensive.
Short walk: Mystras — village and Byzantine site. 4km/2.5mi;

2h (plus visiting time). Easy, but with an ascent/descent of 350m/1150ft. Follow the main walk to the 23min-point, then turn right and follow this small path, keeping right at a fork, to the stream. Cross on stepping stones and follow the path left to a jeep track (33min). Here turn right, steeply uphill, then bear left and climb less steeply. Keep right near a wet patch and you will eventually reach a broad track (53min). Turn right and follow this down to the car park next to the (upper) entrance to the **Mystras site** (1h). At the gate you can collect a site plan which shows you the best way through to the lower gate (*not* shown on our map). I recommend the ascent to the castle and the detour to the Perivleptos, if you have time (add 30-40min). From the lower gate, follow the asphalt road (you can short cut the right bend) back to **Mystras village**.
Alternative walk: See **Alternative walk 18, page 91.**

How many visitors have come to the ruined Byzantine city of Mystras, stood on the hilltop castle and, gazing upwards at the soaring peaks of Taygetus, wondered what is concealed in their many folds and plateaux? The prosaic

Ayia Sofia church in the Byzantine site of Mystras (Short walk)

answer to that is several remote villages, abandoned monasteries, terraced fields, flowery meadows, fir forests and limestone gorges. But the poetic answer is to walk up there and see.

Start the walk from the plane tree in the centre of **Mystras** village: follow the road northwest (towards the BYZANTINE SITE). At the fork in the road with the statue of Constantine Paleologos in the middle (**2min**), fork left and immediately keep left, up STEVEN RUNCIMAN STREET (named after the prominent British Byzantinist). The lane bears right. In front of a large, sand-coloured CHURCH (**5min**) turn left up towards the mountains, and at the end of the lane, continue straight on up the cobbled path (wooden signpost with YELLOW SQUARES). In the cypress grove, follow the path to the right, climbing gently into the lovely mini-gorge below Mystras Hill. Kestrels and falcons wheel from the grey buttress, while butterflies and dragonflies flit around the streambanks. At the wooden SIGNPOST (**23min**), turn left across the concrete water

conduit signed 'TAYGHETI 50MIN' (*but the Short walk to Mystras Castle turns right here*). Pass to the left of the 19th-century chapel of **Ayios Ioannis**, and continue up under the low branches of mixed deciduous woods. When you emerge on the bend of a jeep track (**40min**), turn left and immediately left again (SIGNPOST) up the continuation of the path. Climb steadily through intermittent shade, soon drawing level in height with the castle. A small path joins from the left (**55min**), after which the gradient eases off. The jeep track runs below you on your right. Cross a path and then a stream, then take a gulp from the icy spring of **Kontoyorghi** (**1h10min**).
After crossing the track, the path curls left around a neglected CHAPEL, past a second CHAPEL, and up through nettles to the asphalt road (**1h20min**). There is a

signpost here ('**Taygheti**, alt 700m', plus some optimistic times to Pergandeïka and Faneromeni) and another, slightly warmer SPRING. Turn right and immediately left up a tiny, overgrown path (wooden signpost and waymark — you are now following GREEN TRIANGLES). Keeping right of a big boulder, you pass several ruined houses before reaching a concrete road (**1h25min**), with a well-tended house ahead to the right. Like most Taygetians, The Karounos family winter in Sparta and keep this house, with its cool interior, traditional furniture, sheepskin rugs and wonderful views across to Parnon, as a summer house. The last

permanent inhabitant of Taygeti, a 100-year-old woman, died a few years ago, just after they had asphalted the road to help her relatives look after her!

Turn left and immediately right up the continuation of the path (waymark). A path joins from the left, and both cross the stream (SIGNPOST) and veer right. At the track (**1h34min**) turn right and immediately left up the continuation of the path (SIGNPOST), with the asphalt road visible on your right. When you reach the road (**1h41min**) turn left and, after the right-hand bend, left again up the path (SIGNPOST).

At the next bend the path glances tangentially off the road (SIGNPOST) and climbs to the monastery of **Zoodochou Pigis** (Virgin Mary the Source of Life; **1h50min**). Outside the locked gate are a shady spring and stone benches; inside, if you coincide with one of the Christian scout camps which take place in July and August, you can look round the 17th-century cells and chapel in mid-restoration. From the SPRING follow the marked path up in the same direction (southwest), into open ground. Pass to the right of a white hut and SHEEPFOLD, cross the dirt track and rejoin it (**2h**). Turn right and, after 50m, go left up a signed path, which climbs steeply, bearing right among sparse firs. Where a path joins from the right, keep left (SIGNPOST) and pick up a recently bulldozed track, which completes your ascent to the SADDLE (**2h25min**). To your west loom the sheer flanks of Neraïdovouna peak (2025m), so-called because, in ancient mythology, it was inhabited by mountain nymphs

Top: the ruined Byzantine town of Mystras; below: view over Faneromeni Monastery to Sparta

who on moonlit nights would dance naked around the summit. If any mortal was foolish enough to try and climb up for a closer look, they would dance towards him and kick him off to his death in the abyss below. The original *femme fatale*, or a cautionary tale about a dangerous ascent?

Wild tulips (Tulipa orphanidis)

Detour: If you are feeling energetic (but not foolhardy), you can make a 45-minute return detour up the well-named Xerovouna (Dry Mountain) to your east. On the far side of its flat, 1200m summit lies a panoramic chapel dedicated to Profitis Ilias. A gravelly path leads up the left side of the slope, then bears right in front of a rockface and climbs steeply. At the terraces, contour round to the right and, at the last fir, resume left to reach the brow. Follow the gentle ridgeline east for 10 minutes as far as a grassy dip on your left. The 1160m trig point is ahead to the left, the neglected chapel is off to your right (no frescoes, but a great view over Sparta). Return the same way.

From the saddle, continue along the bulldozed track to a larger track, which leads to a second SADDLE (wooden signpost 'SHELA PLACE ALT 1120M'; **2h30min**). Here turn left along a path which briefly climbs before descending over open, well-signed hillsides. At a fork (**2h40min**) turn right (ignoring the path straight ahead), and take care down the steep, stony stretch. At the track (**2h55min**; SIGNPOST), turn right as far as the right-hand bend, then turn left down a path through Jerusalem sage bushes. In the valley below you lies Pergandeïka hamlet, and beyond it the path winding up to the left of a cliff-face to Faneromeni Monastery. In front of an old THRESHING FLOOR, keep left to the abandoned houses of **Pergandeïka** (**3h 05min**). Turn right between two houses, right again and left to reach a plane tree and the village SPRING. Turn left, fork right (SIGNPOST) and, before an inhabited house (again, the only one), fork right down a small path overgrown with thistles. This crosses a CONCRETE BRIDGE over the plane-lined stream (**3h15min**) and climbs. The first set of zigzags takes you round the foot of a cliff (some loose, rocky sections), the second up to the CREST (**3h 33min**). Follow the part-paved path east through more sage and oak bushes, then wind down to a broad parking area next to the church of **Ayios Stratigos** (**3h45min**). Turn left down the lane to **Faneromeni Monastery**

On the track from Faneromeni Monastery to Sotiros

(**3h50min**), entering through an arched gateway.

There is just one monk, a lively, English-speaking young man called Ierotheos who, if his busy schedule permits, may offer you cool water, Turkish delight and a look inside the recently re-frescoed chapel. He relates that the monastery was founded in the 1840s by Athanasios Ladopoulos, who saw the Virgin Mary in a vision (*faneromeni* means 'made visible') and with her guidance found a miraculous icon in a cave, probably left by an earlier hermit called Pafloutis. The annual celebration falls on the 8th September (Birth of Our Lady).

To continue the walk, retrace your steps through the arches and turn right down a dirt track (BLUE SIGN Μυστράς) towards a rock with a CROSS on it (Pafloutis' Cave is near here). The rough track then bends left and zigzags down into the Langada Valley, with views past Pergandeïka to Neraïdovouna peak. When you finally cross the **Langada Stream** (**4h35min**), you can rest and replenish water bottles by the shady chapel of (**Metamorfosi tou**) **Sotiros** (Transfiguration of Our Saviour). Here, at the wooden signpost with a red-on-white triangle, *leave* the main track and E4 route, and turn right down a smaller track into the plane woods. Follow the TRIANGULAR WAYMARKS across the streambed; the track becomes a path which then follows a concrete-covered WATER CONDUIT. A potentially vertiginous stretch is encountered where this path is cut into the cliff-face; although it is nearly a metre wide and well surfaced, there is a drop of over 50m/150ft to the streambed on your left. Shortly after passing through a cleft in the rocks, the path leaves the conduit and forks left downhill (WAYMARK). After a

brief climb on a stone-built trail, you wind steadily down to a fork (**5h05min**; SIGNPOST).

Here fork left to the cave-chapel of (**Panayia**) **Langadiotissa** (Virgin Mary of the Ravine). The cave is a sublimely peaceful spot, perched partway up the side of the **Langadiotissa Gorge** and looking straight out onto the opposite wall. Within is a tiny chapel, with frescoes from the 14th century and candles (photograph page 15). The dark, dank gorge below is one of the candidates for the *apothetai*, where the ancient Spartans abandoned malformed babies to die — or, I suppose, if they could crawl out of the abyss, to become worthy citizens. Recessive genes, evidently, had not been discovered.

Return the same way to the main path (**5h13min**) and continue left, downhill. You join a gravel track by a small QUARRY and follow it down to the asphalt road in **Parori** (**5h20min**). Turn left for a well-earned drink at one of the charming tavernas on the square, sitting under a huge plane tree by the endlessly gushing springs of Keramos. From here Mystras is an easy 10-minute road walk, following the concrete lane north from the square (ΑΡΧΙΜΑΝΔΡΙΤΗ ΓΟΡΑΝΙΤΗ), then joining an asphalt lane which in turn rejoins the road into **Mystras** (**5h30min**).

Walk 20: MOUNT PARNON — FROM THE EOS MOUNTAIN REFUGE TO MALEVIS NUNNERY

Distance/time: 17km/10.5mi; 5h15min (*excluding* ascent of the Megali Tourla peak)

Grade: fairly strenuous. Although the ascent is short (400m/1300ft) and mostly shady, the descent is long (800m/2600ft), stony and waterless

Equipment: picnic, plenty of water, sunhat and cream, compass and waterproofs (in unsettled weather), phonecard

Transport: 🚌 Car tour 4 passes both the EOS refuge (short detour at 105km) and the nunnery (122km), but you will need a friend to drop and collect you. Otherwise, drive to Ayios Petros and leave your car there (several hotels/pensions), then take a taxi to the mountain refuge, called 'Καταφύγιο ΕΟΣ' (Katafigio EOS) after the Greek acronym for the Hellenic Alpine Club. It is a 15km drive on an asphalted and well-signed road, starting along the road to Astros, and turning right after 3km. Arrange with driver to collect you from Malevis Nunnery (where there is a cardphone).

Shorter walk: EOS refuge — Malavazo. 11km/6.8mi; 3h; moderate, with an ascent of 400m/1300ft and descent of 300m/980ft. If you have a reliable car, driver and map, arrange to be picked up at the dirt road near the Malavazo summit (see map).

This is a wonderful mountain walk with all the sounds and smells of rural Greece: the wind rustling the fir branches, the pungent resin dripping from the pines, the wild herbs brushing against your legs, the distant tinkle of goats' bells. The route starts from the EOS refuge, climbs steadily to a grassy plateau set on an eerie moonscape, and descends through drier, rockier valleys more typical of coastal Greece. It's a perfect escape from the summer heat and crowds.

Start out at the EOS REFUGE (altitude 1420m/4660ft), which is normally locked. Follow the dirt road east downhill (wooden signpost 'MEGHALI TOURLA PEAK, MALEVI MONASTERY'). You pass a huge FOOTBALL PITCH on the right, and the track becomes asphalt. At a right-hand bend (**7min**), turn left down a path waymarked with a RED SQUARE and a red-and-white '33' DIAMOND. You will be following these all the way to Malevis Nunnery. After a few minutes you cross a forest track and continue steeply down the path. At a SPRING and POOL (**17min**), bear left to reach the asphalt road. Turn left along the road, heading towards AYIOS PETROS. After 100m turn right (red square and sign on the left: 'KRONION 3H'); Kronion is

another name for Megali Tourla, Parnon's highest peak. Descend through flower-filled meadows, then bear right into the pine woods (red square). At the VALLEY FLOOR (**30min**) turn right for 100m, then cross the stream (last water until Malevis Nunnery!) and climb across a track up a steep path (waymarks). At an overgrown track (**35min**) turn left and after 100m bear right (waymarks) up a stony streambed. After crossing a fallen tree, clamber up left into a rocky gully and follow it to the right (uphill), as it winds like a natural corridor into the mountain. At the JUNCTION OF GULLIES (**53min**), keep left (waymarks), climbing all the while over steadily improving terrain. At the forest track (**1h10min**) turn left, uphill.

The track crosses the **Kanelia** spur (**1h30min**) — a nice resting point — and contours across the stonier northern flanks of the spur. Keep left along the main track and, where it peters out (**1h36min**), continue up the gully on a stony trail. After a few minutes the trail climbs up to the left (waymarked tree); here turn *right (unsigned)* and immediately left, up a steep path climbing across open ground (RED SQUARES again) and then dropping back to the gully.

At a JUNCTION OF GULLIES (**2h**) keep right; soon you emerge from the forest onto a meadow (**2h 07min**) with a STONE HUT and CORRAL ahead. In spring this is bursting with crocuses, wild-flowers and butterflies, in summer with crickets and mountain tea (*tsaï tou vounoú*). This is a sage-like herb, *Sideritis syriacus*, which grows above 1500m on rocky limestone slopes in the eastern Mediterranean. The Greeks prize it for its digestive qualities, when boiled with water and sweetened with honey. In some mountain villages, where our European (*evropaïkó*) or black (*mávro*) tea is unheard of, this is what you will get if you ask for a cup of *tsaï*. Mt Parnon is famous for its *tsaï* and oregano — so famous that there are signs forbidding commercial picking. No one will mind if you pick a few stalks — choose the greenest buds and let them boil for several minutes.

Follow the jeep track north across the 1700m plateau, a grassy moonscape with the rocky flanks of **Megali Tourla (Mt Parnon)** soaring up to your right. After a while (**2h15min**) you pass a wooden signpost indicating a steep and pathless route up to this summit (1934m), which is only for dedicated peak-baggers. A minute later you can fork right along a faint path over the fields — a short cut to the soon-visible chapel of **Profitis Ilias** (**2h30min**) at the far end of the plateau. The smaller hump of **Mikri Tourla** rises to the right of the chapel — an easier summit if you want to take in the rugged views over the east coast of the Peloponnese to Spetses, Hydra and the Argolid.

From the unlocked chapel (the highest point in the walk), follow the jeep track downhill for 100m, then fork left down a stony waymarked trail. After a few minutes you rejoin the jeep track at a hairpin bend and follow it down for another 100m, before forking left again, this time on a tiny path (inconspicuous waymark) descending steeply over stony ground through pine and fir trees. Keep your eyes peeled for the RED SQUARES, bearing left if in doubt. Eventually (**2h50min**) a broader, needle-covered trail joins from the left and the going improves. You reach a dirt road (**3h**; SIGNPOST) and turn right, climbing gently. After 250m turn left (SIGNPOST) down a stony path, which curls left down a stony slope. After five minutes, don't drop onto the jeep track, but veer right past a shepherd's BRANCH-SHELTER (with guard dog). You cross some open ground towards the rounded summit of **Malavazo** (1503m). In front of the fenced field turn right along a faint track (the official path is slightly higher but don't worry). At a slight RISE (**3h10min**) turn left along a rocky spur following the waymarks. After a few minutes turn right along a stony jeep track until it peters out at a SECOND RISE (**3h18min**). Bear slightly left here, down a faint, stony path through sparse juniper woods. The barren summits of Parthenio and Ktenias are visible ahead. The path bears right while the valley drops off on your left. Then, by a fir tree, it bends left, crosses a fallen trunk (**3h30min**) and plunges left down a slippery slope, before resuming a gentler, right-hand descent to the tree-choked gully. Cross the gully (**3h37min**) to the left bank briefly, then drop back along the gully floor (*no waymarks*). Soon (**3h45min**) you climb the right bank — a RED-PAINTED '24' is the first of many numbers counting you down to the nunnery. There follows a frustrating ascent up a right-hand side gully until you meet a smaller path (**3h55min**) and turn sharp left. At a rock slab on the right (**4h03min**), fork right, uphill, before a second treacherous descent over loose stones. At a heap of boulders and a drystone wall ahead (**4h15min**), turn sharp left (inconspicuous RED ARROW). You pass some wooden TROUGHS; the gradient eases (apart from one sudden, short drop), and the forest dwindles to allow a glimpse of a red-tiled dome below. After another small drop (just under **5h**), there is an unmarked patch of open ground where you must turn right up a small path, rising to a concrete-walled SPRING. Here follow the ARROW pointing left. You pass under a huge plane tree. Aim to the left of the concrete water CISTERN, then go down the left side of a fence.

At the road turn left and walk round the buildings of **Malevis Nunnery** to the CAR PARK at the front (toilets, cardphone; **5h 15min**). If you go through the gates (with shoulders and legs covered), you can pop into the frescoed chapel of the Dormition of the Virgin. The 30 nuns are quite used to crowds of pilgrims who come to the see the miraculous 'myrrh-bleeding' icon.

Distance/time: 13km/8mi; 6h
Grade: moderate: about 600m/ 1970ft total ascent/descent, mostly on well-made, reasonably graded forest paths. There are some rough paths around the stony summit of Stamatira.
Equipment: picnic, plenty of water, suitable clothes for visiting the monastery (trousers/skirt and something to cover your shoulders). *Note:* The monastery is closed from 12.00-16.00, so either leave early or wait till noon to start the walk.
Transport: 🚗 to/from Polydroso (Car tour 4 at 87km). There is no bus service.
Shorter walk: Polydroso —Ayii Anargyri — Polydroso. 8.7km/ 5.4mi; 3h45min; easy, with an ascent/descent of 400m/1300ft. Make a gentler loop by omitting the Stamatira summit.

This is a lovely circular walk, taking in the historic monastery of the 'moneyless saints', the coniferous forests around Polydroso and the rocky, panoramic summit of Stamatira. It is pleasantly remote — you are unlikely to meet anyone en route — without being dauntingly rugged.

Start the walk in **Polydroso**: from the eastern (apse) end of the CHAPEL beneath the school and main square, walk downhill towards 'GOGHENA, STAMATEIRA, VASSARAS'. The lane is waymarked with BLUE SQUARES AND TRI-ANGLES. The former will guide you as far as Stamatira summit, the latter will guide you back via the monastery. Cross the BRIDGE at the bottom of the village (**5min**) — this is where your return route comes in — and go straight on, bearing right uphill. There are good views back to the village and the cave-chapel of Ayios Ioannis (see page 25) behind. You cross an open RIDGE (**15min**), descend to a small gully and climb again. Five minutes later you cross a SECOND RIDGE (from where the white chapel which crowns the Stamatira summit is just visible on a wooded ridge far ahead) and contour through fir forest.
Cross a THIRD RIDGE (**30min**) and descend over open ground, look-ing ahead for blue squares, before re-entering the forest. As you scrunch over the fir cones, passing RED-PAINTED NUMBERS which indicate the distance walked (in hundreds of metres), look out for woodpeckers flitting among the trees. The path climbs to reach a FOURTH RIDGE (**1h**) — open, stony ground with abandoned fields beyond. This is the start of the area called **Goghena**, where the village's wheat and barley used to be grown. Continue across the overgrown terraces, following the blue squares carefully. Soon a BLUE TRIANGLE ON A TREE TRUNK (**1h 15min**) signals the junction of the outward and return routes. *(The Shorter walk turns right here.)*
Keep straight on for the summit ascent and, as you will be return-ing the same way, take a few mental notes as you go. The path climbs gently through patchy forest, with glimpses of the monastery below right. *Attention:* at one point the path turns unexpectedly left (**1h40min**), before bearing right again across a fallen tree (inconspicuous BLUE SQUARES; RED '39' DISTANCE MARKER). If you miss this turn you will find yourself on a fainter trail with faded red paint-splodges, which leads you too far right. Approaching the gentle summit ridge (**1h55min**), fork right (RED

103

Polydroso or Tzitzina?

A village marked as Polydroso on any map is invariably called Tzitzina by locals. Why? Many Greek villages, particularly those in the mountains, were originally given their names by non-Hellenic tribes who settled there during the 7th-14th centuries. In the northern Peloponnese and some Cyclades islands, the Albanians moved peaceably into the mountainous areas, and their descendants still speak a dialect called *arvanítika*. In the northern mainland it was the Vlachs, a semi-transhumant folk of Romanian origins, who occupied the high summer pastures, and who still speak a Latinate language amongst themselves. Here in the eastern Peloponnese, the Tsakonians — about whom even less is known than the other tribes — founded villages based around timber and quarrying industries on Mt Parnon. During the cultural 'purification' of the 1967-74

The old school at Polydroso, now a simple but charming hostel

military dictatorship, every village was given a Hellenic name, usually either a translation of the Slavic term, eg Karia (walnut) for Arachova, or a new, nondescript name, eg Neohori (new village) or a saint's name. Maps were updated, but out of habit locals continued to use the non-Hellenic name, many of which are easily recognised by their -ova, -itsa or -eika endings. The Hellenists chose Polydroso (Much Coolness) for Tzitzina, which is thought to come from the word 'heights' in Tsakonian.

ARROW on a fir tree), go 50m downhill and, by a blue square and RED '45', fork left (uphill) again to regain the ridge. Follow it northwest through patchier forest and rockier terrain. You pass to the right of a huge LIMESTONE SLAB (**2h13min**), and see Veria village and the barren hump of Parnon's 1934m peak (Walk 20) to your right. Brace yourself for five minutes' steep climb, before continuing alongside the boulder-topped ridge. You in fact pass beneath the (unseen) summit chapel before crossing the ridge, turning left, and climbing back up the south slope to reach the

SUMMIT of **Stamatira** and the chapel of **Analipsi** (Ascension; **2h30min**).

There are wide-ranging views over the Evrotas basin, with the town of Sparta in the middle and, behind it, the three massifs of Taygetus: from right to left, the barren summits of northern Taygetus, the twin peaks of Neraïdovouna and Goupata, and the five high peaks of the Pendadhactilo. Vassaras' red rooves huddle below you, while the long, forested spine of Mt Parnon stretches out behind you. The unlocked chapel contains modern frescoes, including a stern

St Cosmas with rosary and crook, proclaiming a damning message of destruction to an empty landscape of barren mountains — not unlike the summit zone of Mt Parnon. Return the same way to the PATH JUNCTION (**3h30min**), not forgetting to bear left (off the ridge) and right again between '46' and '45'; and after crossing the fallen tree ('39') to bear left and right. TO CONTINUE TO THE MONASTERY, turn west downhill, now following BLUE TRIANGLES. After five minutes, a path joins from the left and the surface improves. Ten minutes later you reach a jeep track (**3h45min**) and continue straight on. Soon a wire fence runs along on your right, behind which lies the monastery (looking distinctly unwelcoming). You walk all the way past it before plunging right down a steep path (**3h55min**) to the main dirt road. Here (**3h58min**) turn right to the main gate of **Ayii Anargyri Monastery** (**4h**), where you are reminded not to smoke, take photos or bare your shoulders and legs. The monastery is dedicated to the *ayii anargyri* (the silverless), referring to SS Cosmas and Damion, patron saints of medicine. These twin brothers were unpaid physicians who healed Christians persecuted by Diocletian. They are usually depicted carrying a wooden casket containing coloured powders and surgical instruments, as in these contemporary frescoes by Photis Kontoglou, who also painted the murals in Athens' Town Hall. Their martyrdoms are celebrated on the 1st of July, when pilgrims flock to this monastery seeking miraculous cures.

After your visit, follow the main dirt road back downhill (no waymarks), past a right hairpin bend, to a left hairpin. Here (**4h15min**) turn right on a tiny path (two waymarks). Ignore a trail forking right and, in open ground by the valley floor, turn right along a jeep track, passing a fenced WATER PIT on your right. When the track ends (**4h25min**) follow the path (and a PIPE) up the streambed. You cross briefly onto the left (true right) bank and back again, then find yourself in the streambed, which will only carry water — briefly — after a heavy downpour. Huge plane trees provide welcome shade, but watch out for slippery boulders and holes covered by dead leaves. You pass through old fields (some nettly patches) beneath orange cliffs on the left. The path climbs steeply to the right (**5h**) for a minute or two before dropping back to the valley floor. The stone-walled meadows and walnut groves are now overgrown with bracken, and the mill buildings completely dilapidated. The stream may be flowing, but don't drink from it. Eventually (**5h40min**) you leave the streambed and head up left to a small, cultivated apple orchard, where a wall guides you right and across the stream again. Then you cross the stream for the last time (**5h45min**), climbing a cobbled path to the left, past a chunk of old aqueduct, to a RUINED MILL (**5h50min**). At the bridge familiar from the outward route, turn left up a concrete lane, and after 50m keep straight/right up a path (no waymark) to reach the church and main square in **Polydroso** (**6h**).

Walk 22: LEONIDION • MELANA • LIVADI

Distance/time: 11km/6.8mi; 4h
Grade: moderate, with an ascent/descent of 480m/1575ft. There is little shade, the terrain is rocky, and the path between Pragmateftis and Melana is somewhat unclear.
Equipment: water, sunhat and sunglasses, swimming things. A walking stick is useful for the rocky terrain, and long sleeves for the potentially overgrown sections
Transport: 🚌 to Leonidion (the base for Car tour 4); follow the walk directions to the 13min-point and try to park by Ayii Pantes Church. 🚌 from Athens (five a day), Sparta (once a week) or Tripolis (three a day) to Leonidion. ⛴ hydrofoil from Athens or Monemvasia to nearby

Plaka (up to three a week). To return: 🚌 (Timetables 31, 35) from the road above Livadi to Leonidion, or 🚕 taxi from Livadi (or Melana or Pragmateftis)
Shorter walk: Leonidion — Melana. 7.5km/4.7mi; 3h; fairly easy, with all the climb but no descent); return by 🚌 (Timetable 35) or taxi.
Longer walk: Leonidion — Melana — Sapounakeïka – Paralia Tirou. 23km/14.3mi; 7h30min; strenuous, with an ascent/descent of 800m/2600ft. Follow the dirt road from Melana over the hill of Profitis Ilias (see touring map) and down to Paralia Tirou, catching a 🚌 or ⛴ hydrofoil back.

This is a delightful walk combining well-made mulepaths, aerial views over Leonidion, coastal scenery and the chance to swim at the end. On the way, you pass through Melana, a pretty mountain village of whitewashed, red-roofed houses, where you can stop for a drink or snack. If you start early, you can complete the ascent in the morning shadow, and reach the beach of Livadi for a late lunch.

Start the walk in the centre of **Leonidion:** follow the main road east (towards ASTROS, ATHENS) and, after the square with the taxi rank, turn left and then, before the OTE BUILDING, right. At the STOP SIGN go straight over, and go straight over the next junction. At an oblique junction, keep half left up ΟΔΟΣ ΠΟΛΙΤΗ. Where the HEALTH CENTRE is signed left, keep right. Five minutes up this road you pass the church and cemetery of **Ayii Pantes** on your left (**13min**). Keep going along the gravel track. After two minutes fork right down to the riverbed and up the other side, towards a SHEEPFOLD with a corrugated iron roof. Then, 150m before the sheepfold, at the top of an olive grove, turn right along a path (RED SPOT; **25min**). This curves right, below a rocky outcrop, and zig-zags visibly up the facing slope. It is a lovely old *kalderimi* (stone mulepath) which is still used by

View over Leonidion from the mulepath early in the walk

the goats and their herder. The views back over Leonídion, nestling among russet cliffs, are ample reward for the steady climb.

After 45 minutes you pass a ruined limekiln on your left (**1h10min**), and the path switches to the sunny, south-facing slope. At the PLATEAU (**1h20min**), you join a dirt track and keep straight on in the same direction. Some 100m further on, by a stone SHRINE and CISTERN, keep straight again. Ignore the right turn to Ayii Anárgyri Chapel (**1h25min**), and enjoy the views over the coast to the islands of Spetses and Spetsopoúla.

Soon (**1h40min**) you pass a house on the left and a track leading right to the unseen village of Pragmateftís. 150m past this house, turn left up a small track towards a metal water container, then turn immediately right along a small path. This heads north-northwest over loose stones, skirted by prickly oak bushes and low stone walls. It is unclear at times, but generally flat or climbing very slightly. After a good 10 minutes (**1h50min**) you should reach a left turn into a dry gully; if you have strayed to the right, a smaller path will deposit you back onto the main path. Cross the gully to the far slope, where the pathfinding and surface improves. After 20 minutes (**2h10min**), at a larger group of olive trees, follow the main path which forks right and slightly downhill. You pass a SHRINE, with plunging views over the coast by

107

From top to bottom: Ophrys
spruneri (*Grecian spider
orchid*), Muscari como-
sum (*tassel hyacinth*),
Centhranthus ruber (*red
valerian*)

Livadi. After 25
minutes you reach
the first house of
Pera Melana
(**2h35min**); Pera
means 'yonder',
which is true for this part
of the village if, like most
people, you were to
approach from the north.
At the road, with
railings, bench and
turning area,
continue along the
concrete lane. At a
large house on your left
(**2h38min**), fork left
up a narrow concrete
lane (or you can stay
on the main road for a
more direct route).
The lane ends at a
lovely CHAPEL
(**2h42min**) with a
flower-filled forecourt
and wall-benches partly
shaded by cypresses;
there is a WATER TAP
behind. From the
parking area, continue
along a path and, at
the streambed
(**2h45min**), turn
sharp right down a
steeply descending
path. This crosses
the streambed and
enters the main part
of **Melana**. Follow
a concrete lane
downhill*, then go
left at the junction

(along the flat) and finally descend
some steps to rejoin the road by a
small café/shop with a telephone
(**2h55min**).
From the 'square' take the concrete track down to the right of
the village hall (signed ΚΟΙΝΟΤΗΣ
ΠΕΡΑ ΜΕΛΑΝΩΝ). This becomes
a path and leads to the main
Leonidion–Astros road
(**3h02min**), where you turn right.
After 100m, by a tall eucalyptus
on the left, fork left past a house
with black railings (*NB: not sharp
left which leads to Kisagas Beach*).
This dirt road, passing flower-
speckled hillsides and a few
German-restored holiday homes,
has lovely views over the sparkling
sea. After 25 minutes (**3h27min**),
just after a house on the left and
before the road bends inland, turn
sharp left down a rough track.
After 30m bear right, heading
down into the orange and
mandarin groves. After three
minutes, at the STREAMBED
(**3h30min**), turn left along a
pebble track to reach the SEA
(**3h33min**). It is a pleasant
enough swimming spot, with
shingly stones and shade from a
lentisc tree.
Afterwards, follow the shore to the
right, to the houses of **Paralia
Livadi** (**3h38min**). Turn right up
a concrete lane, passing a café on
the right — if you plan to return
by taxi this is a good spot to call
from. Otherwise continue past the
café and, after 100m, turn left up a
concrete lane. This joins a larger
road and takes you up past **Livadi**
CHURCH to the main road (**4h**) by
the Melina honey/Delicia Brava
FACTORY, where you can pick up a
bus back to Leonidion. There is
also a cardphone here.

---

*For the Longer walk, go
uphill on this lane, past the
highest houses of Melana, to a
dirt road. Follow this left, up

to the hilltop chapel of Profitis Ilias,
then descend past the old villages of
Sapounakeïka and Tiros to the
newer resort of Paralia Tirou.

Walk 23: TRAILHEAD ABOVE LEONIDION • TSITALIA • SINTZAS MONASTERY • LEONIDION

Distance/time: 24km/15mi; 6h15min

Grade: strenuous, with an ascent/descent of 800m/2600 ft. There is little shade and a 3km stretch without proper paths.

Equipment: sunhat and cream, plenty of water, picnic, compass. A walking stick is useful for the rocky terrain, and long sleeves for the potentially overgrown sections.

Transport: as Walk 22, page 106 (park in Leonidion centre). The trailhead is 4.5km above Leonidion, on the road to Tsitalia. Take a taxi and ask for 'to monopáti ya ton Áyio Athanásio'. You are looking for a stone-stepped path climbing to the left, 1km after a right hairpin, and just after a gentle right bend. Or, if you are feeling fit, walk to the trailhead (add 4.5km/1h20min).

Shorter walks

1 Trailhead above Leonidion — Tsitalia. 6km/3.7mi; 2h; easy ascent of 350m/1150ft. Return by bus (Timetable 34).

2 Tsitalia — Sintzas Monastery — Leonidion. 13.5km/8.4mi; 4h 25min; moderate ascent of 450m/1475ft and descent of 800m/2625ft. Take the early bus up to Tsitalia (Timetable 34) and pick up the walk at the 1h50min-point.

Sintzas Monastery

This circuit takes you from the delightful, cliff-ringed town of Leonidion up past a wonderful hilltop chapel, to a forgotten village on a rugged plateau, over an 850m saddle, and down again via the breathtakingly situated monastery of Sintzas. The middle section of the walk crosses featureless, scrub-covered hillsides, which will be hot and unshaded in summer, but it's an inspired approach to the cliff-side monastery. Some route-finding skill is required for the latter part of this, following a barely-used trail through bushy hillsides.

Start the walk at the trailhead described under 'Transport', and follow the stone-stepped path steeply uphill. Where the main path to Tsitalia bends sharp right (**10min**), turn left, contouring to a waist-high IRON CROSS at a saddle. Here, keep left again and curl up the left flank of the steep, stony peak. You should spot some fortifications on the way up, and a ruined building (an old chapel) on the very summit next to the trig point. Drop a couple of minutes down the seaward side to reach the (newer) chapel of **Ayios Athanasios** (**40min**). It is a tiny building, usually open, and perched sheer above the little port of Plaka. The views along the coast towards Poulithra are equally breathtaking.

Return the same way to the main path (**1h**) and continue uphill towards Tsitalia. The goats have created a few short cuts, but they rejoin by a holm oak tree with a SHRINE and a WELL (**1h15min**). After five minutes (**1h20min**), you join a rough jeep track and keep straight ahead. Ignore smaller tracks, including a left fork towards two cypresses, and carry on past a cylindrical fibreglass WATER RESERVOIR, looking like an extra-terrestrial portaloo, and some goats' sheds. Soon (**1h27min**) you reach a slight crest with the houses of Tsitalia visible ahead, and the flanks of Mt Madara behind. At the asphalt road (**1h40min**), by a bench and

huge ΚΑΛΩΣ ΗΛΘΑΤΕ ∇ ΚΑΛΟ ΤΑΞΙΔΙ sign, go diagonally across, along a lane between the school and the cypress-ringed WAR MEMORIAL. At the first houses of **Tsitalia** (**1h44min**), follow the main lane to the right. At the end of the road (**1h47min**), turn left up to the square with benches and playground (cardphone and simple café nearby). In front of the SQUARE (**1h50min**)

turn right down ΚΟΛΟΚΟΤΡΩΝΗ lane. When the concrete runs out (**1h56min**), ignore a left fork and go straight on out of the village. At a blue SHRINE (**1h57min**) a larger track joins from the left; keep straight on, across a concrete BRIDGE, and fork left. Pass a stone WATER RESERVOIR on your right. At a fork (**2h05min**), follow the main track to the right and pass through a small OLIVE GROVE in the otherwise barren scrubland. The track crosses a gully (**2h14min**) and veers right. You are aiming to cross the low hills ahead over the saddle between Sgourias (920m) and Tourla (782m) — ie, just right of dead ahead. Where the track bends sharp left (**2h20min**), keep right/straight on; go through a SAND PIT, cross the gully again and, at a SECOND SANDPIT

(**2h28min**) turn left up a rough track. This bears right, then left, climbing steadily. Just after crossing a gully, where the track levels out ahead (**2h50min**), fork right up a stony path through bushes (tiny RED WAYMARKS) which continues to climb. After 10 minutes you cross a sharp-rocked ridge (**3h**) with spindly, red-barked strawberry trees (*Arbutus unedo*) below. The path descends gently to the head of a small valley. At the disused TERRACED FIELDS (**3h05min**), bear right to the gently V-shaped saddle, choosing the largest of the many small paths.

At the SADDLE (**3h20min**), with Leonidion's east-west gorge ahead, and the ridge of Aetorahi in the foreground, turn sharp left up a path (more waymarks) climbing

Gladiolus italicus *(field gladiolus)*

steadily. Then bend right as the path levels out. Ignore the path forking up left (**3h 26min**), and continue to traverse the right flank of the rocky knoll of **Sgourias**, with its sparse strawberry trees. You reach Sgourias' northern spur by a cement trough and WELL (**3h35min**), with views west along the length of the Parnon range.

From here you need to follow the WAYMARKS AND CAIRNS carefully all the way to the monastery. Paths lead north down this spur for three minutes (**3h38min**) to where the spur levels out. From here bear slightly left, dropping gently between bushes over stony ground — this hardly qualifies as a path. Ahead is the ridge of Aetorahi, with its front of orange-grey cliffs and a small rounded summit on the right; you should aim broadly for its highest point. At one point, about 50m before the bottom of a line of sharp rocks sticking up like teeth, turn left and zigzag down a couple of hairpin bends before continuing towards Aetorahi. The path zigzags once more before continuing parallel to the gully. Where a faint trail joins from the right, you cross the gully on your left (**4h10min**) — you have descended about 150m in height so far. The path improves slightly, heading to the right across a slight spur, before descending in decreasing zigzags. You cross a smaller gully, squeeze through a dense patch of arbutus bushes, then wind down over open ground. The path now bends

112

right through a sheer-walled *GORGE*, across some sandy ground, and winds steeply down the left bank.

Finally **Sintzas Monastery** rears up ahead in the lee of an over-hanging russet cliff (**4h35min**) — a view to compensate any route-finding problems! Enter through the gate on the left, properly dressed (no shorts or bare shoulders). There are two nuns resident here from April to October, and sporadically in the winter. They celebrate the feast day of St Nicholas, to whom the monastery is dedicated, on the 6th December and the previous evening. They are welcoming, particularly to Greek-speakers. Although the building is relatively modern, the icons date from the 17th century, and in the library you can see the spine of a giant snake which was supposedly killed by worshippers using trombones — quite how is left to the imagination! The cave used to shelter a huge fig tree (*sintza* in the local Tsakonian dialect), which is always a sign of fresh water; there is one spring in the monastery and a second below.

From the monastery follow the rough dirt road which winds steeply downhill, with several concrete sections to avoid wash-outs. After about 30 minutes the gradient eases (**5h**) and you approach newly planted apricot and peach groves — these are all fenced round so don't try any short cuts. After a further hour (6km from the monastery) the road, now asphalt, enters **Leonidion** (**6h**). Turn left across one of the bridges to reach the centre (**6h15min**).

Walk 24: FROM PIGADI TO POULITHRA

Distance/time: 10.6km/6.6mi; 3h30min

Grade: fairly easy, with a descent of 550m/1800ft on well-made paths

Equipment: water, sunhat, swimming costume and towel. A walking stick is useful for the rocky terrain, and long trousers for overgrown sections.

Transport: 🚗 Poulithra and Pigadi are accessible via a 10-20km detour from Leonidion, the base for Car tour 4. 🚌 from Leonidion to Pigadi (very early!; Timetable 33). To return: 🚌 lunchtime bus from Poulithra back up to Pigadi (Timetable 33), or 🚌 from Poulithra back to Leonidion (Timetables 32, 33)

Alternative walk: Poulithra — Ayios Georgios — Poulithra. 8km/5mi; 2h20min; a flat and easy circular walk. Access by 🚗 or 🚌 (Timetables 32, 33) to Poulithra. Follow the lane from 'central' Poulithra (ie about 800m inland), signed Αγ Γεωργιος. (If coming by bus, ask for the 'tríti stási'.) The lane drops across a gully, loses its asphalt covering and, after 3km, joins the main walk at the telephone pole (the 2h-point), where you turn left down the concreted track towards the sea. Follow the main walk to the end.

This is a wonderful walk from the remote farming village of Pigadi to the turquoise sea and green carob groves of Poulithra Bay. Farm tracks and old paths make the going easy, and, best of all, it's nearly all downhill. The seaside chapel of Ayios Georgios makes a lovely lunch spot.

Start the walk from the large church of **Ayios Georgios** near the beginning (western end) of **Pigadi**. Follow a small lane northeast, passing a PLAYGROUND and cardphone on your right, and the small cream-coloured chapel of **Ayios Dimitrios** on your left. After three minutes, fork left, passing a blue metal SHRINE on the right. After another three minutes, by a walled house and faded road sign on the right, keep right (more or less straight on). After four minutes, where the concrete lane bends right to the last houses of Pigadi (**10min**), fork left up a jeep track, passing a huge TREE STUMP on the left. After 20 minutes you pass through the tiny hamlet of **Longari** (**30min**; wrongly marked as Soulineika on most maps). At the last houses of Longari keep left, passing a SHRINE on your left soon after. At the end of the dirt track (**45min**), with well-preserved STONE TERRACES to your left, continue straight along a roughly cobbled path heading north. After a gentle climb through abandoned fields studded with wild pear trees, the bay of Poulithra comes into view. The path descends until, about 30 minutes from the end of the track (**1h15min**), it swerves left towards Poulithra and the distant greenhouses of Lakos east of Leonidion. Ignore the much smaller path continuing straight down the ridge here, towards the rocky summit of Aflaouras to the northeast. Instead, follow the well-made stone mulepath descending left towards the sea, passing wild flowers, butterflies and the occa-

sional tortoise (if you're lucky) or snake (if you aren't).

When you reach an OLIVE GROVE (**1h45min**), continue straight ahead along the descending dirt track through mixed olive and carob groves. Some 15 minutes along this, by a telephone pole with boxes (**2h**), turn right down a concreted track towards the sea. (The main track goes straight on here to Poulithra; *the Short walk joins here.*)

After five minutes fork left down a dirt track, past two ruined barns, to a larger, roofed BARN (**2h05min**) — these *apothikes* were used to store carob pods. Besides providing a chocolate-tasting fodder for animals (and humans), locals claim over a dozen uses for these seeds, but are hard pushed to name them (I gather soap and liquor-flavouring are two). The Africans use the seeds inside to measure out precious substances — they all weigh very close to 200mg, which is the origin of our 'carat'.

The onward route to Poulithra lies to your left. But first make for the seaside chapel of Ayios Georgios: follow the track to the right. It becomes a path skirting the upper fringe of the stony beach, passing in front of another small barn, and then following the shore to the left. **Ayios Georgios (2h25min)** is set tranquilly at the water's edge, with a concrete 'quay' and a little shade from a pine tree, but no water or rain-shelter (it is locked). Return the same way to the large CAROB BARN (**2h45min**). Then take the small path leading west, just inland. It goes through a gap in the bushes and into an OLIVE GROVE. From here, you must make your way west, parallel to the sea, across a succession of stony groves — the owner is happy for walkers to appreciate his land! A few pointers: after the first grove, find a break in the fence, and pick up a tractor track. Later, you cross two small, overgrown gullies on tiny paths — or, if there are no waves, you can follow the shingly beach instead.

At the end of **Poulithra Bay** (**3h15min**), take the small but clear path skirting the coast, a few metres inland, through somewhat prickly bushes. This climbs to about 30m above sea level, then descends (**3h25min**) as a rough jeep track to the charming little harbour of **Poulithra** next to the Αποθηκη bar. Turn right for a delightful taverna, turn left and walk five minutes to reach the Hotel Akroyiali, and beyond that the BUS STOP (**3h30min**) on the road from Leonidion to Pigadi.

Poulithra Bay

Walk 25: FROM KREMASTI TO KIPARISSI

Distance/time: 11.2km/7mi; 4h05min

Grade: moderate. Although the distance is not huge, there is over 1000m/3300ft of fairly rocky descent. You should be confident finding small paths in the forest.

Equipment: strong boots, picnic, plenty of water, compass, stick

Transport: 🚗 or ⛴ hydrofoil to Kiparissi. The village lies between Car tours 4 and 5. Call a taxi (from Richia) to take you from Kiparissi to the trailhead east of Kremasti. The walk starts in a valley called Toumbali, 4km east of Kremasti, accessible by a good dirt road. As you approach Kremasti from the south, about 1km before reaching the village (which you can see ahead), turn right on a dirt road by a blue shrine. The road is signed ΠΕΛΕΤΑ and waymarked with a white-on-red diamond '33'. The surface is fine for taxis or hire cars. After 3km there is a sharp left bend, and 800m further on you reach the valley floor. The smaller dirt track to your right is the onward walking route (more diamond waymarks). 🚌 from Molai to Kremasti and back from Kiparissi to Molai (Timetables 27, 28), but using public transport will necessitate a night or more in Kiparissi.

Alternative walk: Kiparissi — Babala — Kiparissi. 16km/10mi; 7h; strenuous. This circular walk avoids transport problems, but the route is tougher (with 1000m/3250ft of ascent/descent), and very hard to find. See walking notes on page 118.

This a wonderful walk combining forested mountains, cliff-side paths and the unspoilt coastal village of Kiparissi. Best of all, you are almost guaranteed solitude, apart from the occasional shepherd. But the hard part is arranging the transport. The best option is to stay in Kiparissi before and after the walk, and use a taxi to reach the trailhead near Kremasti. The descent is quite stony — make sure you have comfortable boots and (preferably) a walking stick. And bear in mind that Kiparissi is in fact three settlements: Vrisi (the highest and oldest), Paralia (where the hydrofoils dock) and Mitropolis (further north along the coast). The walking directions below take you into Paralia, but buses call at all three.

Kiparissi — Mitropolis, the northern settlement along the coast

Start the walk in the **Toumbali Valley**, at the trailhead described above. Follow the track south (DIAMOND WAYMARKS), with burnt pine trees up to your left. The track passes a SHRINE and wooden animal fold on the right, then twists left and right rather aimlessly. When the track ends amidst firs (**30min**), carry on along the well-trodden path, passing a fenced ENCLOSURE on the left, and occasional red spots, arrows and diamond waymarks. After 10 minutes' zigzagging uphill, you reach a beautiful meadow dotted with wild pear trees. Cross the left side of the meadow making for the low point on the forested skyline, and at the far side climb again (faded waymarks) — up a stony slope and past a 4-METRE HIGH TREE STUMP.

At the top (1070m altitude; **50min**) the path descends along the left, then the right bank of a fir-choked gully. After a good 10 minutes, ignore the path forking right to a well (although unsigned, this is the continuation of the '33' route to Harakas). Instead keep left past a fallen tree trunk and above some barrels used as animal TROUGHS (just over **1h**). The path (now fainter) follows a shallow dip, then a gentle spur with intermittent views towards the peak of Mt Pilioura. Dropping down its right flank, you pass some fields and a roofless RUIN on the right (**1h15min**). Stonier now, the path crosses to the right bank of a dry gully, then climbs slightly to a larger clearing — **Makria Lakka** (Distant Meadow). The path leads to a pair of HUTS (**1h30min**) beneath a huge evergreen oak tree, with some fenced troughs, a well with a bucket, and a threshing floor. It's a good spot to rest and examine the grape hyacinths, cyclamen and orchids which abound in spring.

From the THRESHING FLOOR, descend past the fir nearest to the valley (the second fir), then go straight past a third fir and up a stony path with faint red waymarks, including a painted 'ΚΥΠ' and 'K'. After five minutes the path contours to the left (**1h35min**). A further five minutes sees you bearing right across a SADDLE, before 15 minutes' nasty descent over loose stones, tempered by the view of the distant sea. Eventually (**2h**) you cross a gully, where a blue-spotted path joins from the right (from Babala; *the Alternative walk joins here*), and the going improves, though still rocky.

A huge valley opens up on your left, and the path clings to the steep mountainside. After 30 minutes you reach the chapel of **Ayia Varvara** (St Barbara; **2h 30min**), set on a ledge among the cliff-sides, with flat, sun-warmed rocks nearby for a panoramic picnic. The chapel is open, and you can light a candle in thanks for your safe passage so far. A tiny path by the chapel forks right to Palaia Hora (Old Kiparissi), an unlikely cluster of ruins perched on a steep saddle, which was sacked by Ibrahim Pasha and abandoned.

Continue down the main path, passing some black-and-orange overhangs which drip with water in spring. The firs are replaced by low, mixed woods of scrub oak, maple and hazel. Take care with your footing over the scree-covered sections. After about 30 minutes you cross the **Zastano**

117

ridge (**3h**) and Kiparissi comes into view. You can rest in the paltry shade of a carob tree and look up to the huge rocky bulwarks of the mountain whose northern flank you have just crossed. The path — now shadeless — zigzags down through a steep, sparse carob grove. Look out for the switchbacks, and the RED ARROWS which indicate short cuts. After passing to the right of a huge boulder, a fence appears on your left. The path curves left and joins a track with a GOAT BARN to your left (**3h30min**). Turn right, downhill, and enter the olive groves. After the concrete section, keep left at the fork (**3h45min**). At the asphalt road with the bridge and SCHOOL to your right (**3h58min**), turn left and then keep right for **Paralia** (**4h05min**).

Alternative walk: Kiparissi — Babala — Kiparissi

This walk, although WAYMARKED IN BLUE in 2002, should only be undertaken by those with a compass, route-finding experience, and plenty of time in case you get lost!

It will help if you can get a lift to the 45min-point! Follow the road up through **Vrisi** (the highest village of Kiparissi), past a right bend and a left bend below the cliffside chapel of **Panayia sto Vracho**. 100m above this left bend, take a small path forking right, up towards a cubical hut and

Alternative walk: shepherds' hut at Kouskori, and limestone rock stacks above the Babala plateau

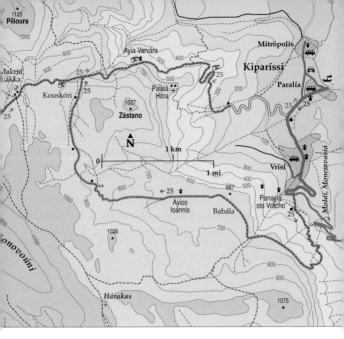

adjacent pole (**45min**).
At the HUT (**50min**), fork right
(old sign, ΠΡΟΣ ΜΠΑΜΠΑΛΑ)
and follow the clear path climbing
southeast. When a small path forks
left to the road (**1h05min**), follow
the main path to the right,
winding steeply and stonily uphill.
The path levels out (**2h**) and veers
right (northwest), beneath an
overhang. You go through a
rickety GATE, then through a
NATURAL CORRIDOR in the rocks,
and reach the plateau of **Babala**, at
650m altitude (**2h20min**).
Follow the small trail, with occasional BLUE WAYMARKs and patches
of stone wall, west-northwest to
the chapel of **Ayios Ioannis**
(**2h50min**). Crossing old fields,
you reach a fork (**3h**) and follow
the blue arrow to the right. There
follows a good hour of steady
climbing, passing weird and
wonderful limestone rock-stacks,
until you come out at a small,
crag-ringed PLATEAU (**4h15min**),
with a well 20m to your right, and
a crumbling stone enclosure on
your left. It's best to keep left

(west) here, along the flat 'field';
then, at the old terrace walls, bear
right (northwest), watching for
BLUE SPOTS. You should cross a
rocky spine by a single fir
(**4h30min**), pass a stone-and-
wood pen near a lightning-charred
trunk, and crest the skyline by a
leaky hut, 950 metres above sea
level (**4h40min**). A rapidly
improving path then descends
north, past some old threshing
floors and the still-used hut of
Kouskori, to join the main walk at
a gully (**5h**). Turn right here and
follow the main walk from the 2h-
point; you've just over 2 hours to
go.

See also photograph on page 8
Distance/time: 4km/3.4mi;
2h40min
Grade: fairly easy, but the last part
of the walk is rocky and trailless —
you need to be agile. Only neat
walking times are shown: within
the town times will be doubled or
trebled by visits and shopping.

Equipment: water, sunhat and
sunscreen, picnic. A walking stick
is useful for the rocky terrain
Transport: 🚗 to/from Monemvasia (the base for Car tour 5);
park near the eastern end of the
causeway. 🚌 from Athens/Sparta
(five a day), ⛴ hydrofoil from
Piraeus/Zea (up to three a week)

There is no better way to explore the wonderfully preserved, fortified Byzantine town of Monemvasia, and the
unique headland on which it sits, than on foot. As it happens,
you don't have any choice. Cars are excluded from the town
centre by a massive medieval gate, the hilltop castle is only
accessible via a steeply zigzagging path, and the rocky
coastline all around is no place to moor a boat. This short,
circular route — one can't really call it a hike, as you are so
near civilisation — is in my view the best way of seeing, within
a day-trip, the town centre, its sea-walls, the citadel and the
rocky coastline that protected it.

Start the walk from the EASTERN
END OF THE CAUSEWAY linking
Monemvasia to the mainland, by
the petrol station and 'Pizza-Grill'.
Unlike the main gate area, there is
plenty of parking here. Follow the
road to the MAIN GATE, the one
breach (hence *mon-emvasia*, single
entrance) in a fearsome wall
running down from the citadel to
the sea. Go through it and follow
the main cobbled alley straight
ahead/slightly left as far as the
CATHEDRAL SQUARE (**15min**), with
its church tower, archaeological
collection and cannons.
Here keep straight on/left and, at
the fork, turn sharp left, uphill —
it is worth climbing the citadel
while it is still cooler. Go around
to the right of a house signed
CAVIN/KABEN, and continue up the
main trail, through the interme-
diary double gates and then the
upper gate into the CITADEL
(**30min**). This is where about
5000 people — the ruling classes
of Monemvasia — once lived, safe
from attack, and dependent on
cistern- and rain-water for their

supplies. Of the countless vaulted,
subterranean CISTERNS, many are
still intact — unlike the houses,
which have all but crumbled away.
The crenellated PERIMETER WALLS
and the two TOWERS at the tips of
this 'acropolis' are also preserved,
as is one beautiful, 13th-century
church; and the best route past
them is as follows.
Turn sharp left, passing the
rooftop of the gatehouse on your
left. After five minutes, fork right,
uphill (left follows the panoramic
perimeter walls, but is a dead end).
At the junction with a larger path
(**40min**), turn left and continue to
climb through giant fennel and
sage bushes. At the next junction,
follow the path left to the WESTERN
TOWER (**42min**; views over the
new town of Yefira) before
proceeding right (east) to continue
the route. The path crosses a
crumbled wall, and then descends
steeply, passing to the right of
some collapsing chambers and
cisterns, to reach **Ayia Sofia**
(**50min**). The only remaining
church of the dozens once adorn-

ing the citadel is a beauty, although, sadly, the unfrescoed but wonderfully acoustic interior is no longer open.

From the olive tree at the church, a good path leads back to the MAIN CITADEL GATE. Before leaving the citadel, you can follow a path left, past the eucalyptus trees, to the eastern (seaward) tip of the rock in about six minutes, returning the same way (**1h02min**).

On the way back down the zigzagging path, shortly after passing through the DOUBLE GATES, you can short cut to the eastern gate of the *kastro* (old town) as follows. Fork left (**1h 10min**) and keep left, passing below a mysterious, white-rimmed door in the cliff (if the suspense is too much, you can climb up to it in a few minutes — it's a charming, single-chambered CHAPEL carved out of the rock). Then continue along the path (**1h 20min**) which follows the foot of the cliff, above the prickly pear and euphorbia trees, to the top of the EASTERN CITY WALL. Wiggle downhill on small paths, keeping 10-20m from the wall, as far as the GATEWAY (**1h30min**). (If the rocky coastline ahead does not appeal to you, you can easily return to the town centre from here by by walking along the sea-wall, passing a tiny swimming jetty en route.)

To continue the main walk, go through the eastern gate and along the path to the LIGHTHOUSE and outlying buildings (**1h35min**).

From here, the route becomes narrow, rocky and, eventually, scrambly. Start along a slight ledge among a jumble of serrated limestone rocks and crevices. Round the corner about 10m above sea level, and a small path materialises, threading through the euphorbia (tree spurge), past a huge CISTERN on the left. It then climbs to about 20m above the sea, soon becoming very hard to follow in the bushy vegetation.

When it fizzles out entirely (**2h**) descend carefully and gently to pass round the base of a huge boulder projecting towards the sea. Stay at this level for a couple of minutes, then descend carefully to sea level and pick your way along the rough rocks. If there is any swell you may get sprayed. Do look up as well, to see Ayia Sofia chapel and the enceinte wall below.

Eventually you reach a rocky ledge just 1m above sea level (**2h 25min**). It's fun to walk along, especially on windy days when you'll be dodging the sea-spray. The ledge deteriorates to a mess of boulders again 150m before the Pizza-Grill (**2h30min**), so I advise cutting up left, past riots of spring *Malcolmia*, and following the wall past a CIRCULAR TOWER, back to the starting point (**2h40min**).

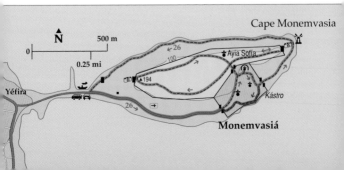

Walk 27: AYIOS NIKOLAOS • VAVILA • AYIA KATERINI • FARAKLO • MESOHORI • (AYIA PARASKEVI CASTLE) • NEAPOLI

Distance/time: 15km/9.3mi; 6h10min (plus optional detour of 0.5km/20min to the castle)

Grade: moderate: after a steep 300m/1000ft climb, the route undulates around the 500m mark before descending, at times steeply, to sea level. The majority is on small, stony paths, with short stretches on dirt road and (at the end) a gravelly riverbed.

Equipment: water, sunhat and sunscreen, picnic. A walking stick is useful for the rocky terrain, and long sleeves for the potentially overgrown sections.

Transport: 🚌 from Neapoli to Ayios Nikolaos (Timetable 29)

Shorter walks: Of the many possibilities, I recommend (1) and (2c).

1 You could catch the Neapoli–Velanidia bus (Timetable 29) to the col of **Vavila** (διασελο Βαβιλας) and join the walk at the 1h05min-point, thereby cutting out almost all the uphill — leaving 13km/8mi; 5h10min to Neapoli.

2 You could cut the end out by catching a bus (Timetable 30), taxi or passing lift from a) **Faraklo**, b) **Mesohori** or c) **Ayia Paraskevi** back to Neapoli, saving about 2h45min/2h/1h respectively. A mobile phone and good Greek would be useful if calling a taxi.

3 There is also a marked trail (Δ1 + Δ5) leading from Neapoli via **Paradisi** to the chapel of **Ayia Katerini** in about 1h30min, making a potentially circular walk; but when I last walked it, the watermill valley below Paradisi was so overgrown that I do not recommend it.

This is a varied and exciting walk, combining a glimpse of the Vatika's wild and rocky highlands with a stroll through two historic, panoramic villages: Faraklo and Mesohori. The ruined Frankish-Venetian castle which once protected them from pirate raids makes a fitting end to the walk, or you can continue all the way into Neapoli.

Start the walk in **Ayios Nikolaos** — a surprisingly extensive village, split in two by a small gully. Where the main road crosses this gully you will see a red sign (Δ8 *AGHIOS NIKOLAOS — KATO KASTANIA*) pointing back north towards Neapoli. Follow the road in this direction for 50m, then turn right up a concrete lane (RED SIGN, RED/WHITE WAYMARK). Where the lane curves left to a church, fork right up a concrete path (waymark) and, at the wider concrete track (**5min**), turn sharp right, climbing steeply up a well-marked path. At the highest house, turn left along a path which winds up through the edge of pine woods, bordered by wild gladioli in spring. At the bulldozed track (**28min**) turn left (*no waymark*), and, where a track joins from your left, keep right. At a larger track (**40min**), turn left (RED SIGN). After 80m, by oleander bushes, turn right (RED SIGN) up a very steep, messy path, which soon clears up and climbs steadily north. Below to your left you can see the chapel of Ayios Stefanos in the lee of a huge boulder. You cross another trail (**53min**) and pass under some TELEPHONE WIRES. Soon (just after **1h**), keep right, uphill, to reach the asphalt road at the PASS of **Vavila** (**1h 05min**), named after the rocky summit nearby.

Turn right and immediately left

Ayia Paraskevi Castle below Mesohori

(RED SIGN) along a dirt track. *Don't be mislead by the waymarks heading up the left road-bank; simply follow the gently descending track.* Keep left at the fork (**1h10min**) and, 80m further on, fork right *(no sign)*. At the next fork (**1h20min**), go left to crest a spur, where the track ends. Keep straight on along a waymarked path, with low-spreading trees to your left. The path descends the right bank of a gully, with rocky outcrops soaring up to your left; then crosses the gully and rounds the base of the lowest outcrop, climbing steadily.

You cross a once-terraced meadow (**1h45min**), where wild garlic, campanula, leopard's bane, tassel hyacinth, vetch, cyclamen and the endemic red 'Goulimi' tulip grow in profusion. Keep right, passing a FINGER OF ROCK. Ahead, the 744m peak of Profitis Ilias, topped by masts and aerials, comes into view. At a red sign (PARADISI 1H; **2h 05min**) fork left. Follow the marked path northwest then west over scrubby hillsides for 25 minutes, to the chapel of **Ayia Katerini** (**2h30min**) and its adjacent dining house, hidden in a grassy bowl within the mountains. There is little shade but the chapel is usually unlocked. Follow the dirt track up out of the bowl, ignoring the path leading left past two upright boulders to Paradisi (see Shorter walk 3). After 12 minutes you reach a ROAD JUNCTION (**2h42min**) heralded by four red signs and one blue one (pointing back to 'Ag Ekaterini 1 KLM').

Turn left down the KATO KASTANIA–NEAPOLI ROAD (although the sign to Faraklo *may* be pointing to the right). At the first bend, fork right (RED SIGN) and descend carefully over the rubble from the road for a couple of minutes, before bearing right along a clear path. This descends slightly, crosses a rocky spur and curves around a gully to a field choked with asphodels and broom in spring (**3h15min**). Here, drop down one terrace and continue to the right, along a path now overgrown with thistles, wheat and overhanging fig and oak trees. Pass below another BOULDER (**3h25min**) and climb steeply to the right, up an overgrown dip, keeping left to reach the edge of **Faraklo**. At the first (ruined) house, turn right past a mulberry tree and follow a concrete path — soon joined by a wider lane —

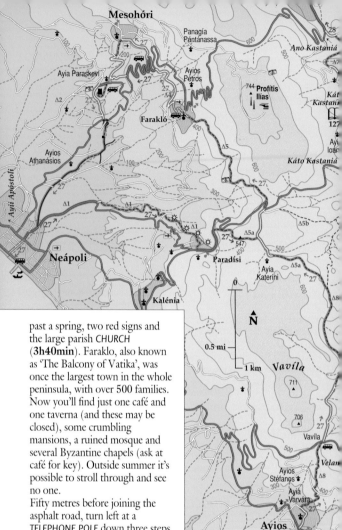

Mesohóri

Panagía
Pántánassa

Ano Kastaniá

Ayios
Petros

Profítis
744 Ilías

Kát
Kastan
127

Ayia Paraskevi

Faraklό

Ayi
Ioáa

Ayios
Athanásios

Káto Kastaniá

Neápoli

Paradísi

Ayía
Kateríni

Kalénia

N

0.5 mi

1 km

Vavíla

711

706

Vavíla

Velan

Ayios
Stéfanos

Ayía
Varvára

Ayios
Nikólaos

past a spring, two red signs and
the large parish CHURCH
(**3h40min**). Faraklo, also known
as 'The Balcony of Vatika', was
once the largest town in the whole
peninsula, with over 500 families.
Now you'll find just one café and
one taverna (and these may be
closed), some crumbling
mansions, a ruined mosque and
several Byzantine chapels (ask at
café for key). Outside summer it's
possible to stroll through and see
no one.
Fifty metres before joining the
asphalt road, turn left at a
TELEPHONE POLE down three steps
and along a marked concrete path.
Bounce tangentially off the road at
the next hairpin bend, following a
concrete lane (RED SIGN and waymark) down past the CEMETERY
and out of the village. Turn sharp
right (**3h55min**; RED SIGN) along
a flat dirt track. The ruined castle
of Ayia Paraskevi is now clearly
visible on a lower hilltop to your
left. At the asphalt road (**4h**

12min) keep left, downhill.*
Just after the first hairpin bend
(**4h17min**) turn sharp right along
a level dirt road (RED SIGN and
blue sign to ΑΓ ΣΩΤΗΡΑ). At a
right bend, with the village of
Mesohori and the church of Our
Saviour just above you (**4h**

*If you want to avoid the very steep
and rough main walk descent below
Mesohori, follow this asphalt road
downhill for a good kilometre (seven

hairpins) and then fork right on a
dirt road (by a blue sign,
ΑΓ ΠΑΡΑΣΚΕΥΗ. You rejoin the
main walk at the 4h51min-point.

25min), turn left opposite a concrete WATER PIPE HOLE, down a steep, concreted path. Keep parallel with and slightly left of the wireless poles. At the THIRD POLE (*easily missed waymark*), bear right, then left along the route of an old path. Where this gets overgrown (**4h40min**), turn left (WAYMARK) past another pole, then continue very steeply down a stony path past lavender bushes. You meet a dirt road at a hairpin bend (**4h47min**). Turn left, past a row of eucalyptus trees and round the head of a gully. When another dirt road joins from the left (**4h51min**; see footnote opposite), keep right, downhill, to another junction, and then go right again (fallen red sign) along a concrete road to the chapel of **Ayia Paraskevi** (**4h55min**).

Detour to the castle (10 steep minutes each way): Fork left on a track through the olive groves, locate a small path to the left of the left-most defensive wall, weave up steeply through lentisc bushes, curl clockwise round the base of the castle and scramble up a thistly pile of rocks through a hole in the southwest corner. Inside the jagged walls is a jumble of collapsed cisterns, vaulted rooms, crumbling walls, and some fine views. Depending on which book you read, this hilltop was either fortified by the Frankish Villehardouins in the mid 13th century after the fourth Crusade, or by the Venetian Loredano in the 1460s after they had retaken the Vatika from the Ottomans in reprisal for the sack of Argos. Either way, it's a fine piece of fortification, which could benefit from some TLC.

From Ayia Paraskevi continue down the concrete road and, 80m after the right-hand hairpin bend (**5h**), turn sharp left down an overgrown path (faded waymark). You soon rejoin the dirt road at a

junction. Here, leave the rather dull Δ2 onward route and turn left along a dirt track, passing between a white hut and a chimneyed house, with dramatic views back up to the castle. At the brow of the hill (**5h10min**), after passing under a telephone wire, keep left along a track which climbs to the ASPHALT ROAD (**5h15min**). To walk all the way on to Neapoli, turn left and immediately sharp right between TWO SHRINES, along a dirt track (not the gated one). Between the first and second telephone poles on the left (**5h17min**), turn sharp left down a disused track, now overgrown with low, prickly shrubs, which winds down to an OLIVE GROVE. Cross this, keeping near its left side and dropping down terraces until you are walking alongside a reed-filled DITCH. At the end of the grove, cross over (or dismantle and remantle) a WOODEN BARRIER (**5h23min**) and take two big steps up, to reach a SHEEP PEN, from where you follow a good track southwest along the valley floor. Where the track crosses a streambed (**5h32min**), turn right along the bed which, after squeezing between some bushes and down a couple of low weirs, becomes a wide, gravelly track. When a track joins from the left (**5h42min**), turn right; after 20m fork left along the continuation of the bed. It's not a particularly pretty route (gravel piles line the banks), but at least it is direct and traffic-free. Soon (**5h55min**) the PARADISI ROAD joins from the left and runs in the bed for 300m, before climbing the right bank. Follow the road along the right bank, past a junction of riverbeds, all the way to the seafront at **Neapoli**, where the Hotel Aïvali is on your right, and the BUS STATION and town centre about 200m to your left (**6h10min**).

Walk 28: VELANIDIA • AYIOS PAVLOS BEACH • KATO KASTANIA

See photograph page 6
Distance/time: 10km/6.2mi; 4h
Grade: easy, with about 300m/ 1000ft of descent/ascent, the former on a jeep track, the latter on stony paths and tracks. Note that the route described is *not* the same as the Δ9 Velanidia–Kastania trail.
Equipment: water, sunhat and sunscreen, picnic. A walking stick is useful for the rocky terrain
Transport: 🚌 from Neapoli to Velanidia (Timetable 29). To return: 🚌 from Kato Kastania to Neapoli (Timetable 30)
Alternative walks:
1 You could continue up to **Ano Kastania** (add 2.5km/1h30min; see map page 124), and catch a bus back to Neapoli from there; but the path ('Δ7') was fairly overgrown at the time of writing.
2 If bus times change, it may be easier to walk this route in reverse.

Of all the beaches in the Vatika Peninsula, the small cove at Ayios Pavlos is my favourite: small, sandy and secluded — accessible only by jeep track and then a short path. As for the trailhead village of Velanidia, its white-faced, red-tiled houses set beneath orange cliffs must be the most picturesque view in the region. Kato Kastania, meanwhile, is a tiny hamlet hidden in a lush valley and forgotten by the rest of the world. A walk combining these three, feasible as a day trip from Neapoli, makes an excellent introduction to the Vatika. Three kilometres below Kato Kastania, incidentally, is an extensive cave called Ayios Andreas, which in 2002 was 'about to open to the public', but apparently has been so for years.

Start out in **Velanidia**: follow the main road back towards NEAPOLI for just over 1km, to the first left-hand hairpin bend, by a '40' SPEED LIMIT SIGN (**15min**). Fork right here down a dirt/concrete track descending past a GOAT BARN. Note that this is *not* the route marked on the Atrapos map (which was barely passable when I visited), but a higher one.
At the fork (**30min**) keep right, down the main track, and at the junction of tracks (where a marked route joins from the right; red sign) keep left, passing a tall-chimneyed HUT on the right. Keep following this track downhill, ignoring any side-tracks. Shortly before sea level (**50min**), you pass a red sign indicating the Δ9 path left to Kato Kastania. Ignore it and follow the track. Just before it reaches sea level, it curls up left to

a FARM (**1h05min**). If the gate locked, you can head right and enter the farmyard at its southeast corner, or skirt round it.
Now locate a rough trail heading east along a slight spur, from the farmyard towards the sea. This disused jeep track peters out in a field (**1h10min**). To reach the chapel of Ayios Pavlos (St Paul) and the quay, turn right here. For the beach, turn left and cross the sparsely-thistled fields to some low carob trees lining the dry riverbed to the north. A small path leads through a gap in the carobs down to **Ayios Pavlos Beach** (**1h 15min**). The water is clear and inviting, but there is no shade.
Return the same way to the FARM (**1h25min**). Cross the yard (you may need to open and close two mesh gates) and follow the path to the right of the house, with the

dry river-gully on your right. The red- and white-waymarked Δ9 path joins from the left (**1h 30min**), and both descend steeply to the dry riverbed and go straight across it. Follow the waymarked path uphill for about 15 minutes. After a flat stretch, a red arrow on a flat rock on the ground points left, steeply uphill. Although this Δ9 route would also get you to Kastania, I suggest *ignoring* the arrow and following the gentler, unmarked path straight ahead. It contours, occasionally dropping a little, round the left-curving spur, before climbing steadily north, with excellent views back over the beach. Loose stones underfoot are a nuisance, but better ascending than descending them. After 40 minutes the path levels off (**2h55min**), and 10 minutes later you join a broad dirt track, with a GOAT PEN down to your right. Follow this track straight on to a T-junction (**3h25min**), where there is a fenced olive grove on your right. Turn left and follow this larger track, bending left, to a junction (**3h32min**) where you turn right. Contouring across the shoulder of a spur, the track bends left and meets the asphalt road at the northeastern edge of **Kato Kastania** (**3h50min**). The cave of Ayios Andreas lies 3km to your right. Assuming it's still closed, turn left into the village proper, which was deliberately tucked into a fold in the valley so as to remain out of sight from pirates. Legend has it that an earlier settlement here, called Megahora and numbering 700 houses, was razed to the ground by pirates and the inhabitants sold as slaves — but not before they had buried their 'golden hen and its golden chicks'. In the VILLAGE CENTRE (**4h**) turn sharp right along a lane (two red signs) if you want the café (easily missed, 100 metres along on the left, with green doors) or the onward route to Ano Kastania. For the Neapoli BUS STOP, carry on to the upper end of the village.

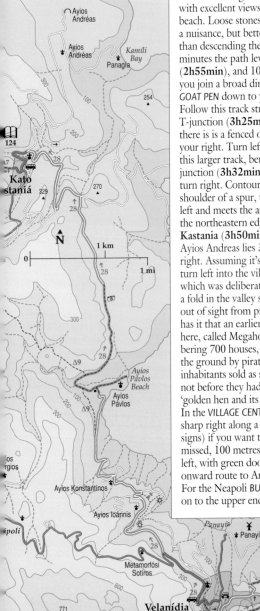

Walk 29: VELANIDIA • CAPE MALEAS LIGHTHOUSE • VELANIDIA

See map on pages 130-131; see photograph on page 34
Distance/time: 16.5km/10.2mi; 6h30min
Grade: moderate, on tracks and stony, but well-marked paths (mostly the 'Δ10'); 300m/1000ft descent/ascent overall
Equipment: plenty of water, sun-hat and sunscreen, picnic, swimming things, including flip-flops (but note that there are better bathing places at Velanidia Beach and elsewhere). Long sleeves are useful for the prickly stretches on the return.
How to get there: 🚌 to/from Velanidia (Detour 2 on Car tour 5); *don't* park by the bus stop/turning point; park further up the road. 🚌 from/to Neapoli (Timetables 29, 30).

Shorter walk: Ayios Thomas — Cape Maleas — Ayios Thomas. 10km/6.2mi; 4h. Access by 🚗: if you don't mind driving on dirt roads, follow the asphalt road down through Velanidia, and at a left bend turn right, signed 'Cape Maleas' in blue and 'Faros' in yellow. The rough dirt road climbs past a shoulder with a ruined windmill (on the walking route). Continue downhill for 1.6km to a red sign, where you park and join the walk at the 1h-point.

The tip of the Maleas Peninsula, with its barren, rocky spine and limestone crags tumbling almost sheer to the foaming blue sea, is a remote place indeed. The only habitation beyond the picturesque mountain village of Velanidia is a small shepherds' settlement at Ayios Thomas, where two families tend goats and catch fish. Beyond that, the only man-made structures are a lighthouse on the northern side and a tiny monastery on the southern cliffs (Walk 30), both uninhabited. The lighthouse has been automated; the monks, who presumably cannot automate isolation and prayer, are building a larger monastery near Ayios Mironas. Between the two, the coast is so sheer that not even Greek path-builders have managed to forge a trail (and don't believe any map that shows one!). The walk follows the old lighthouse-keeper's trail, a route he must have used on a near-daily basis to collect provisions. For variety, the return route from Ayios Thomas to Velanidia follows a lower track, which allows you to see the site (and that's all it is) of ancient Side (pronounced Sídhi).

Start at the BUS STOP above **Velanidia** village: follow the concrete road down past the shop/café O ΒΡΑΧΟΣ on the right. Then (**2min**) turn right up a stepped alley (red sign: AGHIA MARINA 6KM/2H30). After 80m turn right (faded red and white WAYMARK); follow the path to the left, and at the fork keep right uphill. At the SPRING and RESERVOIR, follow the path sharp right, then sharp left.

In the shade of a large tree, keep left and leave the village. By a pretty SHRINE (**10min**) a path joins from the left. Just after this, fork left (where a red sign indicates 'Aghia Marina' to the right) along a lovely flat path carpeted with flowers in spring. This crosses a gully, climbs and descends briefly, before levelling out with fine views of the village and cave-chapel to the left.

In front of a HUT (**30min**), fork left, down to the chapel of **Panayia Dekapentistra** (Virgin Mary the 'Fifteener', presumably because she passed away on the 15th August), which has beautiful views all round. Here, keep right, up the dirt track, to a larger track (**35min**), where you keep left (red sign: LIGHTHOUSE MALEA 6.8KM/ 2H35). At the dirt road with a ruined WINDMILL ahead (**40min**), turn right (red sign) and follow this gently downhill, with the scattered huts and new monastery near Ayios Mironas ahead. A track joins from the right (**50min**), and you reach a RED SIGN just before a junction (**1h**; *the Shorter walk joins here.*) Follow the sign left down a trail, and go left again along the dirt road. A few minutes along, at a left bend, turn right on a narrow path across a small field and immediately follow the broader path left, down a spur, towards an inlet. The descent steepens, and red and white waymarks appear, though if in doubt head for the TELEPHONE POLES. Climb past a large boulder to the first pole (**1h20min**), and follow the line of (wireless) poles all the way to the lighthouse. The path first crosses a tricky slope of loose stones, then heads inland through a gap in the rocks, then levels and broadens out. You pass a GRAFFITI'D BOULDER (**1h45min**) and bear right to see the bleak coastline ahead, dominated by rocky peaks. Despite the apparent harshness, sage, convolvulus, campanula, broom and daisies all find a foothold here, sheltering spiders and huge green lizards, while rock nuthatch, blue rock thrush and quail flit about the sky. The path rounds a small HEADLAND (**2h25min**), and the lighthouse comes into view. After crossing a gully below some ruined STONE HUTS (**2h45min**), you reach the **Cape Maleas** LIGHTHOUSE (dating from the 1860s; **3h**) — rather battered, but offering shelter from sun or wind. You can, at your own risk, climb a spiral staircase past a terrace to the tower housing the light, which is now solar-powered by day and switched on automatically at night. It is frustrating not to be able to continue round the coast, but scramble up a bit and you can, on a clear day, see Milos to the east and Crete to the south. Return the way you came, not forgetting to bear left by the GRAFFITI'D BOULDER, as far as the dirt road by the small field (**5h**). Here turn right (*leaving* the Δ10 trail) and follow the road gently downhill. After 25 minutes (**5h25min**) you pass the turn-off right to the modern chapel of Ayios Georgios, situated on the probable site of the Mycenean town of Side, named after the daughter of Danaos. Nothing has been found here to confirm the theory. Continuing straight on, the dirt road climbs inland for 15 minutes to a right-hand bend (**5h40min**), where it heads back down towards the sea. Here, fork left on a path climbing a steep gully overgrown with broom and lavender. At a left bend (**5h 50min**), fork right on a gently descending, equally overgrown path. At the next fork (**5h55min**), turn right if you want to rejoin the track to the beaches of Kalevolo (1km) or Panayia (2km) and be picked up there. For Velanidia, keep left (uphill). Ignore a small path forking right (**6h**). Climb some concrete steps and join a track (**6h05min**), which you follow uphill. A few minutes later, join a larger track by a blue and white SHRINE, and keep right. When you meet the asphalt road that runs down through **Velanidia** (**6h20min**), turn left to reach the VILLAGE CENTRE (**6h30min**).

Walk 30: AYIA MARINA • AYIA IRINI • AYIA MARINA

Distance/time: 11km/6.8mi; 4h30min
Grade: fairly easy: half on dirt tracks, half on a narrow but well-maintained path, undulating between sea level and 100m/330ft. You must have a head for heights.
Equipment: plenty of water, sunhat and sunscreen, picnic. A walking stick is useful for the rocky terrain, and a windproof jacket in case the sea-wind gets up.
Transport: 🚌 to/from Ayia Marina (Detour 3 on Car tour 5); or taxi (see **Alternative walk** on page 132)

Cape Maleas is sometimes called *to mikro ayio oros* (the small holy mountain), in contrast to Mt Athos, a very large and very holy mountain in Chalkidiki (northern Greece). The comparison is a little optimistic, there being on Athos over 20 (occupied) monasteries and an extensive network of trails, while here there is just one (empty) monastery and a single path to it. Nevertheless, the scenery has something in common: a rugged coastline capped by rocky peaks falling steeply into a foaming blue sea, with only the seagulls for company. This walk follows that single path (initially a vehicle track) to Ayia Irini Monastery, and returns the same way.

Start the walk at the chapel of **Ayia Marina** (park on the northern, shady, side if possible). There are three red signs here, one to Velanidia, one to Profitis Ilias, and one to the MONASTERY OF SAINT IRENE 5.5KM/2H15. Follow this last sign, heading northeast along a dirt track. There are two tracks off to the right (**3min, 8min**), both leading to the (disappointing) PETRIFIED FOREST, which consists of a few knee-high rock stumps, some fossilised shells and a perfect handkerchief of smooth sand for swimming off. Leave them for your return, and follow the main track straight on. At the junction in a dry GULLY (**10min**), keep right (*no* red sign, though you soon pass a waymark), passing above a small pirates' cove. On your left are bizarre, almost Cappadocian rock formations dating from the Pliocene Era. When a track joins from the left (**30min**), continue straight on. After another half-hour, fork right along the smaller track (RED SIGN; **1h**).

Ten minutes later, shortly before the track ends, fork left up a path (red sign: MONASTERY ST IRENE 2.3KM/50MIN). The path, maintained by the community of Ayios Nikolaos for the benefit of pilgrims, climbs past a steep-sided spur, then descends to cross a gully at sea level (**1h30min**). You round the base of another sheer spur and climb steadily for 20 hot minutes, before dropping steeply to the gate of the **Ayia Irini Monastery** (**2h**). The white-washed church of St Irene is a few minutes further on; its roof holds is a rainwater cistern, but the pump may not work, so hopefully you have plenty of drinking water. Pine trees offer shade and shelter from the wind. Up to your left are the cells, which can be used as simple overnight accommodation if you have collected the key in Ayios Nikolaos. Here too is a cistern (and a bucket when I was last there, but don't count on it), a basic toilet, and, nearby, the crude shelter of Osios Thomas, which makes camping look like 5-star luxury.

Serious hermits can continue to the semi-ruined chapel of **Ayios Georgios**, 10 minutes further on (ignore the path descending to the boat landing stage) at the very tip of **Cape Maleas** (**2h15min**). Here you can admire the eyeless frescoes of local saints and the remains of a medieval TOWER and large CHURCH, before gazing out at the endless expanse of blue and meditating on the life of those devoted ascetics who eked out an existence here. Both George and Thomas of Maleas passed into Orthodox hagiography, the former becoming a saint, the latter an *osios* (holy man) — which explains why

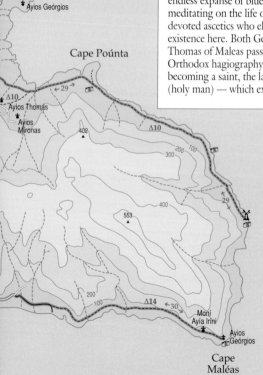

these forenames are so popular here. You can see the island of Kythira to the southwest, the Mani Peninsula to the west, and a motley array of tankers, hydrofoils and fishing boats plying the waters in between. The cape, with its vicious winds and currents, has had a ferocious reputation among sailors since Odysseus was blown off course to the mythical land of the lotus-eaters. Strabo advised you to 'forget about your family if you decide to sail round it'. The monks survived on alms from troubled sailors who sheltered here.

Tumbling cliffs prevent you walking further round the cape towards the lighthouse (Walk 29), so retrace your steps the way you came, remembering to keep left (lower track) after an hour and a half (**4h**).

If you do swim just below Ayia Marina, keep your goggle-eyes peeled for traces of an underwater Mycenean or Minoan city. The Cretan supply station of Minoïtes is thought to be here, as well as the classical temple of Poseidon or Apollo mentioned by Pausanias. Wandering around, you come across square-cut rockbeds, ruts in the stone, and embedded shells — but please remember that it is an offence to take these geological treasures home as souvenirs.

Alternative walk: Ayia Marina — Profitis Ilias (4km/2.5mi; 1h30min. Fairly easy. If you took a taxi to **Ayia Marina** and now find yourself 'stranded', follow route Δ13 to the fishing hamlet of **Profitis Ilias**, from where you can usually get a lift to Ayios Nikolaos (or telephone for a taxi from Neapoli). The route runs along the rocky windswept coastline, passing the hidden inlet of Kleftavlako, where pirates slaughtered and concealed their victims (amphoras full of old florins were found here) and the rather disappointing Cave of the Nymphs.

The monastery of Ayia Irini

BUSES

The bracketed numbers ('+30min' etc) after a town indicate the approximate journey time from the point of origin to that town (including stopping/waiting time).

Buses are a reliable way of getting about

Messinia region

Central office in Kalamata: (27210 22823 or (27210 28581; also www.ktelmessinias.gr)

1   Kalamata – Mavromati (ancient Messene, +1h20min) – Kalamata 05.45•, 14.05•

2   Kalamata – Pylos 05.00•, 06.45, 09.30, 10.45*, 12.00•, 13.00, 15.15, 18.00*, 19.45

3   Pylos – Kalamata 6.45•, 8.00•, 9.00, 11.00, 13.00•, 14.15, 15.30•, 18.00, 21.30

4   Pylos – Yialova – Nestor's Palace – Hora – Gargaliani (+30min) – Hora – Nestor's Palace – Yialova – Pylos (+1h) 7.00•, 9.00•, 11.00, 13.15•, 16.30, 19.30

5   Romanos – Petrohori – Pylos 14.30

6   Kalamata – Artemisia (+50min) – Sparta (+1h50min, change in Artemisia) 09.15, 14.30

7   Sparta – Artemisia (+1h) – Kalamata (+1h50min, change in Artemisia) 09.00, 14.15

8   Kalamata – Sotirianika turn-off (+25min) – Kambos (+35min) – Kardamyli (+50min) – Stoupa (+1h) – Ayios Nikolaos (+1h10min) – Thalames (+1h20min) – Itilo (+1h40min) 05.15*, 07.30, 13.15, 17.00. The 07.30 and 13.15 buses connect at Itilo with onward buses to Areopolis and Gythion (Timetables 16, 18)

9   Kalamata – Karveli (+30min) – Lada (+45min) – Karveli – Kalamata 05.00†, 14.10†

10 Itilo – Ayios Nikolaos (+30min) – Stoupa (+40min) – Kardamyli (+50min) – Kambos (+1h05min) – Sotirianika turn-off (+1h15min) – Kalamata 07.15*, 09.15, 15.15, 19.00

11 Kalamata – Kardamyli (+50min) – Exohori (+1h30min) – Kardamyli (+2h) – Kalamata 05.15 (Sat: 05.45), 13.10•

12 Kalamata – Prosilio – Tseria (+1h) – Prosilio – Kalamata 05.00 (Tue and Fri), 14.40 (Tue and Fri)

13 Kalamata – Kardamyli – Stoupa (+1h) – Saidona – Milia (+1h30min) – Saidona (+2h) – Stoupa – Kalamata 05.15•, 13.10

Laconia region

Central office in Sparta (27310 29921 or (27310 26485; in Gythion (27330 22228; in Neapolis (27340 23222; in Areopolis (27330 51229; also www.ktel-lakonias.gr

14 Gythion – Kastania (below Yiatrissa, +1h) – Gythion 05.30=, 14.10=

15 Areopolis – Pirgos Dirou caves (+20min; waits further 1h30min to collect visitors) – Areopolis (+2h10min) 11.00

16 Areopolis – Itilo (+30min) – Areopolis 09.00, 13.45

17 Areopolis – Pirgos Dirou – Vamvaka – Mina 12.45• (Sat: 10.00)

18 Areopolis – Gythion (connection to Sparta) 08.00, 13.00, 15.10, 17.10

19 Areopolis – Nyfi – Kokkala – Layia (+1h15min) – Kokkala – Nyfi – Areopolis 05.45■, 13.45

---

*not Sat/Sun; •not Sun; =only Mon and Fri; #only Wed; †Mon, Wed, Sat only; ■only if there are passengers for this stop

20 Areopolis – Stavri – Gerolimenas
    – Alika⁺ – Vathia* (+1h) –
    Marmari# – Vathia* – Alika* –
    Gerolimenas 13.45

21 Areopolis – Gerolimenas direct
    13.20, 19.30

22 Gerolimenas – Areopolis 06.45,
    14.30, 16.30

23 Sparta – Kalivia Sohas
    (+30min) – Sparta 07.20*,
    11.00*, 13.40*, 19.20*

24 Sparta – Paleopanayia –
    Xirokambi (+20min) –
    Paleopanayia – Sparta 06.20•,
    07.30, 09.30•, 10.30•, 11.30•,
    12.30•, 14.00, 15.30•, 19.10•,
    20.20

25 Sparta – Ayios Ioannis – Anavriti
    (+30min) – Ayios Ioannis –
    Sparta 06.50, 13.15 (Mon, Sat
    and possibly Thur)

26 Sparta – Mystras (some continue
    to upper gate) (+15-20min) –
    Sparta 06.50, 07.20, 08.45,
    10.00, 11.00, 12.30, 13.45,
    15.00, 17.10, 18.45, 20.20

27 Molai – Kremasti (+1h) – Molai
    05.00=, 13.40=

28 Kiparissi – Molai 05.45 (Mon,
    Wed, Fri), return at 13.40

29 Neapoli – Velanidia (+35min) –
    Ayios Nikolaos (+1h10min) –
    Neapoli 06.15, 12.30

30 Neapoli – Mesohori (+15min) –
    Faraklo (+25min) – Ano
    Kastania (+45min) – Kato
    Kastania (+1h) – Ano Kastania
    (+1h10min) – Faraklo
    (+1h30min) – Mesohori
    (+1h40min) – Neapoli 06.00,
    12.30

Arcadia region

Central office in Tripolis (2710
230140;
also www.ktelarkadias.gr)

31 Livadi (Melina Delicia Brava
    factory) – Leonidion 14.15
    (school term), 16.00 (school
    holidays)

32 Leonidion – Poulithra
    (+20min) – Leonidion 11.00*,
    15.30 (Sat only), 20.15

33 Leonidion – Poulithra
    (+20min) – Pigadi (+45min) –
    Poulithra (+1h30min) –
    Leonidion 05.45 (Tue, Wed, Fri
    only), 13.30*

34 Leonidion – Tsitalia (+30min) –
    Leonidion 06.45=#, 13.30=#

35 Paralia Tirou – Melana (main
    road, +15min) – Livadi (main
    road, +20min) – Leonidion
    07.15, 09.15, 11.30, 15.00,
    19.30 (all times are approximate,
    as buses come from Athens/
    Astros)

TAXIS

For larger villages, the phone
number for the taxi rank or central
office is given below. Where there
are only one or two taxi drivers in a
village, his name and home number
are given.

Kardamyli – Stoupa area
Platsa (Mr Voteas) (27210 74497
Prosilio (Mr Georganteas) (27210
73433 or 73382
Stoupa (27210 77477

Areopolis area
Areopolis (27330 51382 or 51588
54232

Others
Ayios Petros (Mr Karamatzanis)
    (27920 31344
Gythion (27330 23400 or 22601
Kalamata (27210 26565 or 21112
Leonidion (27570 22372
Neapoli (27340 22590
Sparta (27310 24100 or 25300
Richia (27320 51222 or 51333

BOATS

Elafonisos – Pounta (+20min) –
    Elafonisos (+40min) (car ferry)
    07.15, 09.15, etc until 19.15 (or
    17.15 in winter)
Elafonisos – Pounta (+10min) –
    Elafonisos (+20min) (passenger
    launch) 08.00 to 18.00 hourly
    (restricted in winter; (27340
    61177)
Pylos – Golden Beach – Pylos
    (shuttle boat) regular departures
    in summer (no timetable)

*not Sat/Sun; •not Sun; =only Mon and
Fri; #only Wed; †Mon, Wed, Sat only;
■only if there are passengers for this stop

☀ Index

Geographical names comprise the only entries in this index; for non-geographical subjects, see Contents, page 3. A page number in *italic type* indicates a map; **bold type** refers to a photograph. Both may be in addition to a text reference on the same page.

Aï Liás (peak of Mt Taýgetus);
  see Profitis Ilías
Alíka 21, 80, *81*, 82
Alýpa (part of Nýfi) 20, 23
Amýkles 16
Anavrití 13, 16, *91*, 92
Ano Boularíí 80, *81*
Ano Kastaniá (Vátika) 126, 127
Anóyia 16
Arcádia Province 24-6, 106-115
Archángelos (beach) 27, 29
Areópolis 13, 18, 20, 23, 71, *73*
Artemísía 13, 15, *46-7*, 49
Astros 24, 26
Ayia Iríni (monastery, Vátika)
  29, *130-1*, **132**
Ayia Kateríni (near Neápoli)
  122, 123, *124*
Ayia Kyriakí (Máni) 21, 78, *79*
Ayia Marína (chapel, Vátika)
  27, 29, *130-1*, 132
Ayia Paraskeví (castle, Vátika)
  122, **123**, *124*, 125
Ayia Sofía (village and chapel
  above Kardamýli) 59, *60*
Ayia Várvara (chapel near
  Kiparíssi) 117, *118-9*
Ayii Anárgyri (monastery) 103,
  104-5
Ayios Andréas (cave, Vátika) 28
Ayios Geórgios (chapel near
  Anavrití) *91*, 92
Ayios Ioánnis (cave-chapel near
  Polýdroso) 24, 25
Ayios Ioánnis (cave-chapel near
  Velanídia) 27, 29
Ayios Nikólaos (also called
  Selinítsa) 67, *68-9*, 70
Ayios Nikólaos; see Síntzas
  Monastery
Ayios Nikólaos (Vátika) 29,
  122, *124*
Ayios Nikólaos (village and
  castle, Vardoúnia region)
  19
Ayios Níkon (mountain and
  village) 18
Ayios Pávlos (cove, Vátika) 28,
  126, *127*
Ayios Pétros 24, 26
Ayios Thomás (chapel near
  Velanídia) 128, 129, *130-1*

Babála (plateau) 116, *118-9*,
  118
Dafnórema (gorge) 11, 45, *46*
Dekoúlou/Dekoúlon (monas-
  tery) 18, 71, 72, *73*
Díporo (near Geroliménas) **21**,
  81
Divári Lagoon **10-1**, 12
Dríalos 20
Egiés 13, 17, 18
Elafónisos Island 27, 29
Eleohóri 67, *68-9*, 70
Elíka 27, 29
Ellinikoú 27
Elona/Elónis (monastery; see
  Panayía Elona)
Episkopí (village and church,
  Máni) 21
Episkopí (near Koróni) 12
Exohóri 19, 59, *60*
Faneroméni (monastery) *91*,
  95, *96*, **97**, **98**
Farakló 28, 122, 123, *124*
Finikoúnda 12
Fonéas/Foniás (cove and beach)
  18, 64, *66*
Gaïtsés 13, 14
Geráki (Byzantine site, town)
  24, 25
Geroliménas 20, 22, **80**, *81*, 82
Ghólas (monastery) **86**, *87*
Giálova; see Yiálova
Giátrissa (monastery); see
  Panayía Yiátrissa
Golden Beach 10, 40, *42*, 44
Gýthion 13, *17*
Hárakas Tower 22, **84**, *85*
Hóra 10, 12
Ithómi (mountain) **37**, 38
Itilo 71, *73*
Kalamáta 13, 14
Kálives (near Kardamýli) 14,
  59, *60*, 61
Kalívia Sohás 13, 16, *91*, **92-3**,
  94
Kámbos 13, 14, 53, *55*, **56**
Kardamýli 13, 14, 18, 19, 53,
  55, 58, 59, *60*, 63, 64, *66*
Kariovoúni 18
Karvéli *46-7*, 48, **49**
Kastaniá (Vátika); see Ano
  Kastaniá, Kato Kastaniá

Kastánia (Vardoúnia region)
  19, 27
Katafighiótissa (monastery); see
  Panayía Katafighiótissa
Katafígio (part of Tséria) *60*, 61
Káto Karvéli *46-7*
Káto Kastaniá (Vátika) 28,
  126, *127*
Kelefá (village, castle) 23, 72,
  73
Kiparíssi **116**, *118-9*
Kokkála 20, 23, 75
Kokkinóyia 22, 83, **84**, *85*
Koróni 10, 12
Koskárakas (river, gorge) 14,
  50, *52*, *54*, 55
Kosmás (village, pass) 24
Kótronas 20, 23
Koumoustá 13, 16, 86, *87*
Kremastí 116, *118-9*
Krialiánika *73*, 74
Krithína (mountain) 28, *131*
Kynoúria (region); see Arcádia
Lacónia Province 13-29, 71-
  105, 116-132
Ladá *46-7*, 48, 49
Lákki *76-7*, 77
Langáda (village) 18, 75, *77*
Langáda (pass, stream, gorge)
  15, *96*, 99
Langadiótissa (cave-chapel,
  gorge) 13, **15**, 16, *91*, 95,
  96, 99
Láyia 20, 23
Leonídion 24, **25**, 26, 106,
  107, 109, *110-1*, 112
Leontákis 80, *81*, **82**
Liméni 18
Lirá 27
Livádi (Paralía Livádi) 106, *107*
Lykáki (monastery) 59, *60*
Magne, Grande/Maina (castle)
  78, *79*
Malavázo (mountain) 100-*102*
Maléas, Cape **34**, 128, 129,
  130-1
Malevís (nunnery) 100, *102*
Málta *55*, 57
Máni Peninsula
  Outer Máni 13-19, 50-70
  Inner (Deep) Máni 20-23,
  71-85

Maráthi (beach) 10, 12
Marmári (village and beach) 22, **23, 84**
Mavrinítsa (hamlet and spring) 53, **54**, *55*
Mavrománti 37, *38*, 39
Mavrovoúni (mountain, Taýgetus) **19**
Megáli Toúrla (summit, Mt Párnon) 100, 101, *102*
Mélana 106, *107*, 108
Mémi (beach) 12
Mésa Hóra (part of Nýfi) 23, *76-7*
Mesohóri 122, **123**, *124*
Messene/Messíni (site) 37, *38*, **39**
Messínia Province 10-19, 37-70
Methóni 10, 12
Mézapos 21
Miliá/Mileá 13, 18, 67, *68-9*, 70
Mína 21, *76-7*
Mitrópolis; *see* Kiparíssi
Monemvásia **8**, 27, 120, *121*
Mountanístika 22, 90, 81, *91*
Mystrás (Byzantine site, village) **13**, 15, **95**, *96*, **97**, 99
Navaríno Bay 11, 42
Neápoli 27, 28, 29, 122, *124*, · 125
Néo Itilo (also called Tsípa) 18, 71, *73*
Nestor's Palace 10, 11, **40**, *41*, 43
Nomitsís 18
Nýfi/Nýmfi 23
Odigítria (chapel) 20, 21, **79**, *79*
Oriní Meligoú 26
Paleopanayiá 16
Paliókastro (castle) *42*, **43**, **44**
Páliros 83, *85*
Panarítis (beach) 27, 29
Panayía Elona/Elónis (nunnery) 24
Panayía Katafighiótissa (monastery) 16
Panayía Yiátrissa (monastery) **19**, 67, *68-9*
Paradísi 27, 28, 122, *124*
Paralía (east coast); *see* Kiparíssi
Paralía Romanoú; *see* Romanós
Paralía Tiroú; *see* Tirós
Parálio Astros 26
Párnon/Párnonas (mountain range) 24, 25, 100, 101, *102*
Paróri 91, *96*, 99
Passavá (gorge, castle) 17
Pedinó (part of Tséria) *60*, 61
Pendadháctilo (ridge, Taýgetus)
Pépon (village and valley) 22, 80, *81*, **82**

Pergandéika 95, *96*, 98
Petalídi 10
Petrohóri 40, *41*
Petrovoúni **64**, *66*
Pigádi (near Leonídion) *113*, 114
Pigádia (near Kalamáta) 50, 51, *52*
Pigadiótiko (bridge) 50, 51 **52**, *52*, 54
Pírgos Diroú 20, *73*
  Sea-caves 20, 71, *73*, 74
Pláka (near Leonídion) 7, 24, 104, 110
Plátsa 18, 134
Polemítas (part of Mína) 21
Polýdroso (also called Tzítzina) 24, 25, 103, **104**, *104-5*
Pórto Káyio 20, 22, 83, *85*
Poseidon (Temple of) 83, 84, *85*
Poúlithra (town and bay) *113*, 115
Proástio 19, 64, 65, *66*
Profitis Ilías (chapel near Gaítsés) 50, **51**, *52*
Profitis Ilías (chapel near Petrohóri) *42*, 44
Profitis Ilías (peak, Mt Taýgetus) **63**, **64**, 88, **89**, *90*
Profitís Ilías (mountain, Vátika) 28, *130-1*,132
Prosílio 14
Pýlos 10, 12, 45
Rasína Valley 86, *87*
Refuges
  EOS refuge at Arnómousga (Mt Párnon) 24, 100, *102*
  EOS refuge (Ayia Varvára, Mt Taýgetus) 88, *90*
Ríglia, Káto *68-9*, 70
Ríndomo/Ríntomo (canyon) 49, 50, 52, 54; *see also* Koskárakas (gorge)
Rómanos (village, beach) 10, 11, 40, *41*
Sangiás (mountain) 20, 74, 75
Sapounakéika; *see* Tirós
Síde (site, Vátika) 128, 129, *130-1*
Sidheróportas (monastery) *46-7*, 48
Símos (beach, Elafónisos Island) 29
Síntzas (monastery; also called Ayios Nikólaos) 24, **109**, *110-1*, 112
Skoutári 20, 23
Sohá **15**, *91*, **92-3**, **94**
Sotiriánika 14, 53, 55
Sotíros (chapel near Itilo) 13, 18, **72**, *73*

Sotíros (monastery; Viros Gorge) **59**, *60*, 62
Sparta (Spárti) 13, 16, **97**
Stamatíra (mountain) 103, *104-5*
Stávri 20, 21, 78, *79*
Stavropígio 14
Stoúpa 13, 18, 19
Taínaron (ancient city) 84, *85*
  Cape 20, 22, 83, *85*
Taygéti (village) 95, *96*
Taýgetus (mountain range) **4**, 13, **15**, **50**, **51**, *52*, 88, *90*
Thalámes 18, 75, *77*
Tigáni, Cape 78, *79*
Tirós/Tirosapounakéika 24, 26, 108
Tragána 40, *41*
Trípi 15
Tséria 59, *60*, 61
Tsikália 80, *81*, 82
Tsitália 109, *110-1*
Tzítzina; *see* Polýdroso
Vaidénitsa (monastery) 13, 19
Vámvaka 20
Vardoúnia/Vardounohória 13, 19
Vassiliki (forest) **19**
Váthia 20, **22**
Vathý (bay and beach near Páliros) 83, 84, *85*
Vátika Peninsula **6**, 27-9, 122-132
Vávila (mountain, pass) 28, 122, *124*
Velanídia (Vátika) **6**, 27, 28, 29, 126, *127*, 128, 129, *130-1*
Virós (gorge) **59**, *60*, 62
Voidokiliá (bay and beach) 10-11, 40, *41*, **42**, 43
Vório (part of Gaítsés) 12, 48, 50, *52*
Vrísi (east coast); *see* Kiparíssi
Xirokámbi 13, 16
Yámia 12
Yeroliménas; *see* Geroliménas
Yiálova 10, 11, 45, **46**, *46*
Yiatréika (part of Tséria) *60*, 61, **63**
Yiátrissa monastery; *see* Panayía Yiátrissa
Zágha (beach); *see* Mémi
Zahariás (part of Tséria) *60*, 61
Zarnátas (castle) 14, 53, 55, **56**, **57**
Zoodóchou Pigís (monastery) 95, *96*, **97**